Dedication

This book is dedicated to all those exciting participants in workshops and to graduate students at the Universities of Massachusetts and South Florida for their support, enthusiasm and wisdom; and to our colleagues who supported the idea of **Intuition: An Inner Way of Knowing,** especially Frank A. Barron, John C. Gowan, J. P. Guilford, Donald W. MacKinnon, and E. Paul Torrance.

William Beery, The University of Georgia

*I would go without shirts or shoes,
Friends, tobacco or bread
Sooner than for an instant lose
Either side of my head.*

Rudyard Kipling
Kim

BD
181
.S42
1989

Intuition
An inner way of knowing

DORIS J. SHALLCROSS & DOROTHY A. SISK

Poynter Institute for Media Studies Library

MAR 7 '90

Copyright © 1989
Bearly Limited
Buffalo, New York 14213

All rights reserved. No part of this publication may be reproduced, stored in a retrieval system or transmitted, in any form or by any means, electronic, mechanical, photocopying, recording or otherwise, without the prior written permission of the publishers.

Printed in the United States of America
ISBN 0-943456-30-4

Every effort has been made to locate the copyright owners of material reproduced in this book. Omissions brought to our attention will be corrected in subsequent printings. Grateful acknowledgment is made to publishers, authors, and other copyright holders for their permission to reprint material.

Frontispiece	Artwork courtesy of William Beery, The University of Georgia.
Page 13.	Mandala reproduced from *The Right-Brain Experience* by Marilee Zdenek. Copyright© 1983 by M. Zdenek. Reprinted by permission of McGraw-Hill Book Company, publishers.
Pages 14, 16.	Excerpts from the *Meditators Manual* by Simon Court. Reprinted by kind permission of Thorsons Publishing Group Ltd., Northants, England.
Page 18.	*Eidetic Parents Test And Analysis* by Akhter Ahsen. Published by Brandon House, Inc., P.O. Box 240, Bronx, New York 10471.

Pages 19-22, 94.	From *The Intuitive Edge* by Phillip Goldberg. Copyright © 1983, Phillip Goldberg. Published by Jeremy P. Tarcher, Inc., Los Angeles, California. Reprinted by permission.
Pages 31, 32.	Excerpts from *Lucid dreaming: Directing the action as it happens* by S. La Berge in the January 1981 issue of *Psychology Today*. Reprinted with permission from *Psychology Today Magazine*. Copyright© 1981, APA.
Pages 34, 35.	Excerpts from *How To Think Creatively* by E. Hutchinson. NY: Abingdon Press, 1949.
Page 43.	Excerpt from *Anatomy Of Reality: Merging Of Intuition And Reason* by Jonas Salk. Copyright© 1983 by Jonas Salk. Published by Columbia University Press, New York City.
Pages 45, 46.	Excerpts from *Growing Up Gifted* by Barbara Clark. Copyright© 1979, Merrill Publishing Company, Columbus, Ohio. Reprinted by permission.
Pages 49, 93.	Excerpts from *Awakening Intuition* by Frances Vaughan, NY: Anchor Books, 1979. Reprinted by permission of DOUBLEDAY.
Page 50.	Excerpt from *Life Of Mozart* by E. Holmes. Copyright © 1932 by J. M. Dent & Sons, Ltd., London, England, publishers.
Page 51.	Excerpts from *Talks With The Great Composers* by A. M. Abell. Garmisch-Partenkirchen, Germany: G. E. Schroeder-Verlatz, 1964. Reprinted by permission of Philosophical Library.
Page 51.	Excerpt from *The process of inspiration* by Jean Cocteau. In B. Ghiselin (Ed.), *The Creative Process*, NY: Mentor Books, 1952. Reprinted by permission of Librairie Plon, Paris, France.
Page 52.	Comments by Edith Sitwell reprinted from *The Saturday Evening Post. Copyright*© 1958, The Curtis Publishing Company.

Pages 5, 53, 97, 98   Excerpts from *The Tao Of Physics* by Fritjof Capra. Copyright © 1975, 1983. Reprinted by arrangement with Shambhala Publications, Inc., 300 Massachusetts Avenue, Boston, MA 02115.

Pages 64, 65.   Excerpts from *Handbook Of Innovative Psychotherapies* by Raymond Corsini (Ed.). Copyright© 1981 by John Wiley & Sons, Inc., publishers.

Page 80.   Excerpt from *The Inevitability Of Patriarchy* by Steven Goldberg. Copyright© 1973 by Steven Goldberg. Published by William Morrow & Company, Inc., New York City.

Pages 92, 104.   Quotations from *Psychosynthesis* by Roberto Assagioli, with permission of the Berkshire Center for Psychosynthesis, Inc.

Pages 94, 95, 100.   Excerpts Copyright© 1980 by Marilyn Ferguson. From *The Aquarian Conspiracy*. Published by Jeremy P. Tarcher, Inc., Los Angeles, California.

Page 101.   Excerpt from *Conceptual Blockbusting* by James L. Adams. Reprinted by permission of Addison-Wesley Publishing Company.

Pages 102, 103.   Excerpts from *Intuitive Management* by Weston H. Agor, Ph.D. Copyright© 1984 W. H. Agor. Reprinted by permission of Prentice-Hall, Inc., Englewood Cliffs, New Jersey, publishers.

Page 105.   Excerpt reprinted by permission of Common Boundary, 7005 Florida Street, Chevy Chase, Maryland 20815.

Contents

Foreword ix
Acknowledgements xii
A Word About the Book xiii

CHAPTER ONE | What is Intuition?
1

CHAPTER TWO | Research and Efforts in Understanding and Assessing Intuition
9

CHAPTER THREE | Developing and Increasing Intuition
25

CHAPTER FOUR | Children and Intuition
41

CHAPTER FIVE | Intuition in the Creative Arts
49

CHAPTER SIX | Intuition and Psychology
55

CHAPTER SEVEN | Intuition in the Sciences and Mathematics
67

CHAPTER EIGHT	The Myth of Women's Intuition **79**
CHAPTER NINE	Spirituality and Intuition **91**
CHAPTER TEN	Accepting Your Intuitive Self **101**
	Index **108**

Foreword

Which came first, logic or intuition? Can not logic be intuitive? Can not intuition be logical? What is the relationship of sensory data to intuition? Are the two really opposites? Are women more intuitive than men and men more something else? Does intuition fade or flower with age? Are there some things we can know only through intuition, and never through logic?

These are the beguiling questions that lie behind this wonderfully reasonable and down-to-earth book. The authors draw from the study of psychology, philosophy and religion, as well as education, the natural sciences and art, to guide us in understanding this complex area of study. They extract from their experience as teachers and clinicians to provide examples and anecdotes that speak to the practitioner, and to those who apply intuition in their work with children, youth, and the handicapped. Their suggestions are immensely practical. The result is a book that is readable, challenging, and thought-provoking in the pursuit of answers to questions about intuition.

The authors have daringly tried some definitions to fit the facts of inner experience and scientific insights into the creative process. They have given us a compendious set of statements drawn from the Greeks and Romans, Hindu philosophy and psychology, Chinese and Zen Buddhism, Aristotelian poetics and Thomistic scholasticism, and the early empirical psychologies of Helmholtz, Freud, Jung, Jaensch, and the Gestaltists of the early 20th century. They have assiduously farmed the fields planted by Brewster Ghiselin in his noteworthy 1950 collection *The Creative Process*. The authors have drawn relevant examples from the self-reports of Mozart, Nietzsche, Poincare, Max Ernst, and Picasso, all the way to the picture-based intuition of the structure of DNA by Watson and Crick.

Practical applications are addressed in the how-to section of the book, applying Jung's technique of active imagination and the many exercises developed in autogenic training (all heirs of the rich patrimony of Mesmerism). The result is an exercise manual designed to increase intuition in ordinary folk. The exercises could be easily imported into the schoolroom and made into new curricula, or used to enrich training in any curriculum in which intuition may go hand-in-hand with logic and sensory data in building knowledge.

A noteworthy feature of this book is its emphasis on positive rather than negative feelings and expectations. A certain amount of faith is necessary if you are to trust your intuitions in the face of "reasonable" considerations that work against it. Most essential, the authors say, is a spirit of affirmation, with meditation to "quiet the mind," so that you may let your higher self know that you are there, no matter how bedeviled you may be by the project of the ego. "Tear up your list of negatives," they advise.

Evaluation also gets its due in an interesting taxonomy of intuition that lists, as expected, discovery, directionality (sixth-sensing the way to go), prediction, and illumination. Rarely is intuition treated as part of the act of criticism. The authors are willing to examine that neglected aspect of intuition: the ability to rely on the yet unspoken in order to spot superficiality, a concealed lack of deep form, or a mistaken shaping. This valuable extension of the range of intuition to an area of thinking where it often seems foreign forms one of the most fascinating features of this book.

Of course, it is finally up to the reader to make something of a book. My own intuition is that this book will gain a wide audience and influence those readers to apply intuition in ways they never have before. Education is ready for such applications. So is psychotherapy and innovation in business and government. So are, perhaps, even the social institutions that combat enslavement to drugs and alcohol, or crime, poverty, and the abusive guns, both great and small.

Perhaps this is asking a lot of a book that seeks simply to examine intuition as a sometimes-neglected human function. But writing a book is like shooting an arrow into the air: no one knows where it will fall. Intuition is a topic with wings.

Frank Barron, Ph.D., Sc.D.
University of California
Santa Cruz, California

Acknowledgements

Many people have assisted us directly and indirectly in the preparation of this book. We are appreciative to Angelo M. Biondi who first accepted the concept and encouraged us.

Among others who assisted from time to time and in different ways were: Pauline Atkinson, who typed many drafts; Hilda Rosselli and Julie Maloney, who assisted in searching out resources.

The ultimate purpose of **Intuition: An Inner Way of Knowing** is to further the understanding of the role of intuition in the arts and sciences, and the understanding of the inner mind as a way of becoming fully functioning persons.

We offer this book with the hope that its purpose will be at least partially fulfilled.

A Word About the Book

In just a few recent years, more discoveries have been made about how people learn than ever before. Scientists have explored the ancient mysteries of the mind: how we remember things we haven't thought about for years; how we reason; how we make intuitive leaps; whether we think in words or images; how we solve problems; and what truly creative people do in their chosen fields. These topics have intrigued us for years. In this book we share some of this new and intellectually-stimulating material with you. We want to encourage thought, research, dialogue and wonderment about the working of the inner mind.

A secondary reason for writing the book is to answer the critics that belittle intuition and relegate it to a position of unimportance. We bring the topic to you both as a cognitive science to share the systematic inquiry, and as a wonder and a mystery.

This book is about the leaps of imagination of past creative geniuses; yet it should solve the mystery of the inner way of knowing with practical techniques that show you how to stimulate your own intuition.

The first chapter, "What is Intuition?" is followed by one on research efforts and assessing intuition. "Developing and Increasing Intuition," examined in Chapter Three, is intended as a practical guide based on our personal experiences and investigations. Chapter Four deals with intuition in children: the notion that all children are intuitive and society's role in encouraging or discouraging intuitive thought. The following three chapters address the role of intuition in the creative arts, psychology, and science and mathematics. Research, investigation, and personal information is shared to explore the profound impact intuition has had in these three areas. The chapter on the "Myth of Women's Intuition" discusses how women have been viewed by society in the past and in the present, and the effect on their intuitive thinking. In the chapter on "Spirituality and Intuition," we examine the relationship between religion and human consciousness, drawing on the literature of subjective inner experiences and spirituality. The last chapter, "Accepting Your Intuitive Self," invites you to prize your human consciousness and to consciously begin or continue the process of developing your intuition.

This book was an opportunity to explore a topic of great personal and professional interest to us and to share the results of observing, interviewing, and reading about the inner ways of knowing. The importance of intuition for the world culture is tantamount to questioning future development of creative resources using our total consciousness. This book examines investigators from a wide range of fields and concludes that, if we make radical changes in our beliefs about human capacity, we can break through to a new way of life.

Doris J. Shallcross, Ed.D. & Dorothy A. Sisk, Ed.D.

CHAPTER ONE

What is Intuition?

What lies behind us and lies before us are small matters compared to what lies within us.

Ralph Waldo Emerson
Essays

There are some things that you just *know* that you know. We experience reality within our own minds; this phenomenon isn't new to humankind. In fact, our ancestors paid much more heed to the inner knowing that today we call intuition. This inner way of knowing, or intuition, is different from the knowledge gained through experience or from phenomena outside of ourselves.

In the minds of ancient people, there was a clear-cut division between the external stimulus and the internal impression. That is, knowledge that came from inside ourselves was considered of equal importance to knowledge gained through outside sources. As Nel Noddings and Paul Shore (1984) report in *Awakening the Inner Eye: Intuition in Education,* visions or insights among ancient people were looked upon as functions of great importance. The seer or oracle was always a prominent member of the community. Intuitive insights or experiences were regarded as sources of knowledge, as messages from the gods, or as evidence of the seer's exceptional power.

To the classical Greeks and Romans, both rational (analytical, logical reasoning) and intuitive knowledge were valid. In fact, intuition was believed to be special; it frequently superseded rational conclusions. Noddings and Shore (1984) suggest that the entire philosophical school of idealism flowing from Plato is based on the notion that intuition is a reliable source of knowledge. Idealism contends that only mental reasoning is knowable; therefore, reality is essentially spiritual or mental.

Aristotle believed that thought consists of images. Such images have the power to evoke emotions that reveal inner knowing. He stated that intuitive reasoning graphs the first principles. He termed intuition a leap of understanding, a grasping of a larger concept unreachable by other intellectual means, yet fundamentally an intellectual process.

Buddha taught that intuition, not reason, is the source of ultimate truth and wisdom. It follows then that, in Zen meditation, the discriminating conscious mind is quieted and the intuitive mind is liberated, as the meditator seeks truth and wisdom. In Eastern philosophy, intuition is considered a faculty of the mind which develops during the course of spiritual growth.

In the Meditation Schools of China and Japan – "Ch'an" in China, "Zen" in Japan – emphasis is placed on candid searching. Competent instruction awakens into an experience and insight that defy explanation through rational speech. To the aspiring Buddhist monks, this awakening is a revelation of their inner truth and wisdom.

For the Hindu, intuitive insights are achieved through meditation and disciplined control of the mind. Intuition usually illuminates universal cosmic issues, not concrete problems. Intuitive experience is linked closely with spirituality and aesthetics. One aim of Yoga, as practiced by the Hindu, is the systematic development of intuition. Intuition is considered a stable, reliable function of higher levels of consciousness from which a wide range of information is accessible.

Carl Jung, one of the more influential psychologists of modern times, drew attention to the role of intuition in intellectual functioning. He stated that information is received in two ways: (1) externally, through the five senses and (2) internally, through intuition. To help in understanding the difference, it can be put this way:

When *sensing*, you
  – perceive with the five senses
  – attend to practical and factual details
  – are in touch with the physical realities
  – attend to the present moment
  – confirm attention to what is said and done

– see "little things in everyday life"
– attend to step-by-step experience
– let your eyes tell your mind

When using *intuition,* you
– perceive with memory and association
– see patterns and meaning
– project possibilities for the future
– imagine or read between the lines
– look for the big picture
– have hunches or ideas out of nowhere
– let the mind tell the eyes (Sisk & Shallcross, 1986)

Levels of Intuitive Awareness

Frances E. Vaughan (1979), in *Awakening Intuition,* provides an overview of intuition. She says that the broad range of intuitive human experience falls into four distinct levels of awareness: physical, emotional, mental and spiritual. Although these levels of experience often overlap, they are usually easy to categorize according to the level at which they are consciously perceived. Mystical experiences, for example, are intuitive experiences at the spiritual level; as such, they don't depend on sensory, emotional, or mental cues for their validity. Intuition at the physical level is associated with bodily sensations, at the emotional level with feelings, and at the mental level with images and ideas.

The Physical Level

Intuitive experiences at the physical level produce bodily sensations similar to the "jungle awareness" that alert primitive people to possible danger. This awareness is different from instinct, which is unconscious. Jungle awareness can be experienced in a city when certain situations cause you to shiver or to have a stomachache or a headache. Such bodily responses, or cues, reveal information concerning yourself and your environment. Vaughan suggests that tuning in to what the body is telling us can help us make decisions about the situations in which we find ourselves. If, for example, a specific situation consistently makes you tense, you can choose to avoid the situation or make appropriate changes to ease the tension. Paying attention to physical intuitive cues can make a significant difference in how you relate to your environment. Make a list of physical reactions that you have experienced, while driving, or at work, for instance. Are there some that occur over and over again in similar circumstances? Are such circumstances tension producing? If so, what changes might you make to ease these situations?

The Emotional Level

On the emotional level, intuition becomes conscious through feelings. Vaughan describes the emotional level of intuition as being sensitive to other people's "vibes" (vibrations of energy), such as immediately liking or disliking someone or something with no apparent justification, or having an inexplicable and vague sense that you should be doing something. Jot down experiences where you felt sensitive to other people's vibrations of energy. If possible, check this out with the others involved as to whether or not they experienced the same thing.

Intuitive cues on the emotional level often involve relations with other people and seem to take on an almost telepathic quality. Have you ever telephoned a friend or relative who was just about to call you? (One co-author frequently experiences this with her mother who lives a few hundred miles from her.) "Woman's intuition" (discussed later at length), is on the emotional level of intuitive awareness. Traditionally, society was tolerant of women openly expressing emotions but not of men doing the same. This allowed women more freedom to experience self-awareness.

The Mental Level

The mental level of intuitive awareness often becomes apparent through images, or through what might be called "inner vision." Because intuition on the mental level is associated with thinking (although all types of intuition are rooted in the mind), it is most often linked with problem-solving, mathematics and science (but not limited to those fields). Intuition on this level can be recognized when suddenly there is order where there had been chaos. This can occur in a flash or after long, arduous work. Western cultures tend to value the latter approach. First there occurs an exhaustive application of logic and reasoning, followed by a subsequent intuitive flash. This approach is associated with the discovery and invention involved in technological progress. Remember the times when you worked long and hard on something and the solution seemed to come to you "out of the blue?"

Educated guesses that we make, or the formulation of hypotheses and new theories, fall into the category of intuition on the mental level. Einstein was an advocate of taking "intuitive leaps" in the formulation of new theories. In *The Universe Within,* Morton Hunt (1982) quotes psychologist Donald Norman on the subject of intuitive leaps:

> *We leap to correct answers before there are sufficient data, we intuit, we grasp, we jump to conclusions despite the*

lack of convincing evidence. That we are right more often than wrong is the miracle of human intellect.

Fritjof Capra (1977) in *The Tao of Physics* notes the important part that intuition plays in scientific thought and discovery:

> *The rational part of research would, in fact, be useless if it were not complemented by the intuition that gives scientists new insights and makes them creative.*

Capra speaks of "spontaneous insight" as being analogous to "getting" a joke.

We can take an intuitive leap; we can work long and hard with rational processes and then experience a solution in a flash of insight; or we can choose to "sit on it" (or sleep on it). Incubation can be a valuable asset to an intuitive process. Incubation gives the mind time to let a chaotic disarray fall into a pattern of order. Sid Parnes, a researcher and consultant in creative problem-solving, calls it "letting it happen."

Whatever path or paths you follow for utilizing the mental level of intuitive awareness, it is important to continue its nurture to insure that we do not lose one of our most precious assets. In *The Intuitive Edge*, Phillip Goldberg (1983) states:

> *When we mistrust (intuition) or let it atrophy by persisting with exclusively rational-empirical thought patterns we end up tuning in with mono to a stereo world.*

The Spiritual Level

The spiritual level of intuitive awareness is associated with mystical experience and, at this level, is "pure." According to Vaughan, *"Pure, spiritual intuition is distinguished from other forms by its independence from sensations, feelings, and thoughts."* Spinoza, a noted philosopher, defined spiritual intuition as the knowledge of God. Frances Vaughan relates, philosopher James Bergenthal equates this knowledge with man's experience of his own being and says that man knows God through his deepest intuitions about his own nature.

In yoga, spiritual intuition is known as soul guidance. It emerges spontaneously when the mind is quiet. Spiritual intuition is the basis from which all other forms of intuition are derived. Activating spiritual intuition means focusing on the transpersonal rather than on the personal realms of intuition. The personal and the transpersonal can be considered as two modes of knowing or as two different levels of consciousness. In Western thinking, the personal is the ordinary waking state of consciousness in which the world is perceived as objects and events existing separately in time and space. The transpersonal means "beyond the personal." In transpersonal consciousness, the underlying oneness of the universe becomes apparent, and the ordinary confines of time and space are experientially transcended. Both of these realms of human function are available to us. Reason is the mode of knowing appropriate to the personal level. Intuition is the mode of knowing appropriate to the transpersonal level. We need to accept both, expanding our understanding and experiences of consciousness to include both.

Functional Types of Intuition

It is beneficial to examine another way of organizing how you might think about intuition. Phillip Goldberg (1983) categorizes six functional types of intuition: discovery and creativity, evaluation, operation, prediction, and illumination.

Discovery Intuition is similar to discovery in its revealing nature; but where discovery reveals singular truths, facts, or verifiable information, the creative function of intuition generates alternatives, options or possibilities. Ideas generated may be factually right or wrong, but will be more or less appropriate to the situation. Similar to a brainstorming session, creative intuition produces a quantity of ideas from which the ideal solution can be selected, while discovery intuition reproduces the single answer sought in a more factual situation, such as, "what is the structure of the DNA model?" The single "right" answer comes in a flash of knowing.

Evaluation intuition signals "yes" or "no" when one is confronted with choices. Goldberg (1983) distinguishes between rational analysis or intuition in making evaluations, using an example from Tom Duffy, a financial planner who states: *"I might make contingency plans on the basis of a formal analysis of technical data, but the actual decision – to commit or hold off or abandon – is a question of timing, and for that I look to my feelings."*

At times, logic may dictate a move in one direction, but intuition urges another. A friend of ours still keeps on his dresser the ticket for an airplane trip that "something inside" told him not to take, even though it was an important business trip. The plane crashed and all its passengers were killed.

To stimulate your evaluation intuition, try this: Do a logical analysis of an upcoming event (The Super Bowl, Academy Awards). Based on your analysis, predict the outcome. Then, ignoring your rational decision, play your hunch on the outcome. Later, check out your results.

Operation intuition acts like a sense of direction, steering us this way or that. Where evaluation intuition works when there is something to evaluate, operation intuition most often precedes anything specific, kind of nudging you towartd or away from a situation. The situation may be potentially dangerous or perhaps a major positive turning point in your life. This type of intuition is sometimes referred to as a lucky accident, or being in the right place at the right time, or responding to a gut feeling without much information to go on, or coincidence. Think back on your recent experiences. Is there anything that you can attribute to a lucky accident?

Prediction intuition allows us to predict what might happen in the future. We form hypotheses, we foresee future events, we forecast outcomes of situations. Predictions can be warning devices or positive feelings about future activities, or hunches that help us to organize or time these future events. For example, we might exercise extra caution in driving a car because prediction intuition may warn us of possible impending danger. Or we may feel pleasantly anticipatory toward attending an event, not knowing ahead of time that we will see someone there for whom we really care.

Illumination intuition is similar to what Frances Vaughan (1979) calls the spiritual level of intuitive awareness. It has been called, in other places, according to Goldberg (1983), samadhi, satori, nirvana, cosmic consciousness, self-realization, or union with God. Understanding illumination intuition helps us understand all forms of intuition; cultivating it simultaneously cultivates the other functional types of intuition.

Creativity and Intuition

Intuition is considered by many as both the first and the most necessary stage of creativity. In *Intuition: How We think and Act,* Tony Bastick (1982) says that intuition is followed in scientific and mathematical creativity, and in creative problem-solving, by logical verification of intuition. Donald MacKinnon (1962), a well-known researcher on creative personality (writing on "The Nature and Nurture of Creative Talent"), states that *"creativity involves an elaboration of the initial novel insight so that it is adequately developed."* MacKinnon identifies this as a criterion of creativity. D. K. Simonton (1975), a psychologist engaged in creativity research, conducted an experiment on the relation of intuition versus analysis to creative problem-solving. His results indicate that highly creative people improve in their ability to solve problems under the instruction to intuit, and low creative type people improve their problem-solving ability under the instruction to analyze.

John C. Gowan, psychologist and researcher in creativity, also reported that the creative experience involves the intuitive process. He suggested that a relaxed atmosphere that encourages free association tends to lead to altered states of consciousness. In these altered states, our capacity to move from conscious control to a preconsciousness would enhance intuitive processing.

If creativity is what separates us from other animals in our world, then we must awaken and sharpen that initial spark of creativity – intuition.

The value of discovering and enhancing intuitive abilities is lauded throughout the chronologies of history by humanity's greatest thinkers, from both the East and the West. Intuition affects us on every level of our actions, in every relationship we experience – in ourselves, in human affairs, in spiritual affairs, and in cosmic connections. Intuition is the core of who and what we are.

References

Bastick, T. (1982). *Intuition: How we think and act.* NY: John Wiley & Sons.
Burtt, A. E. (Ed.). (1955). *The teachings of the compassionate Buddha.* NY: Menta Books.
Capra, F. (1975). *The tao of physics.* Berkeley, CA: Shambhala.
Goldberg, P. (1983). *The intuitive edge.* Los Angeles, CA: Jeremy P. Tarcher, Inc.
Gowan, J. C. (1975). Trance, art, and creativity. *Journal of Creative Behavior, 9* (1), 1-11.
Hunt, M. (1982). *The universe within.* NY: Simon & Schuster.
MacKinnon, D. W. (1962). The nature & nurture of creative talent. *American Psychologist, 17* (1), 484-495.
Noddings, N. & Shore, P. J. (1984). *Awakening the inner eye: Intuition in education.* NY: Teachers College Press.
Simonton, D. K. (1975). Creativity, task complexity, and intuitive versus analytical problem-solving. *Psychological Reports, 37* (2), 351-354.
Sisk, D. A. & Shallcross, D. J. (1986). *Leadership: Making things happen.* Buffalo, NY: Bearly Limited.
Vaughan, F. E. (1979). *Awakening intuition.* NY: Anchor Books.

CHAPTER TWO

Research and Efforts in Understanding and Assessing Intuition

Man as a spiritual being possesses a capacity for wisdom which is infinite, a resource of happiness which is startling.

Paul Brunton
The Secret Path

We know from experience that our consciousness can undergo extreme alterations, including heightened inner awareness and knowing. When it comes to the criteria of science, however the borderlines are not so easily defined or assessed.

The concept of exceptional ability – such as lightning calculation, eidetic images, remote viewing and Eureka experiences – challenges the adequacy of existing scientific models of human function and individual beliefs about the limits of personal capability. More research, and a rich data base, will help illuminate the nature, mechanism, and scope of these exceptional abilities.

However, a field of consciousness research, unavailable twenty years ago, does exist; and the outlook for continued development is positive. Sperry, the 1981 Nobel prize laureate in neuroscience, stated that recent conceptual developments in the mind/brain sciences are clearing the way for a rational understanding of these higher abilities.

This chapter examines various concepts about the intuitive experience such as "flow" by Csikszentmihalyi (1975), revisits Spearman's three principles of cognition and explores intuitive experiences as adaptive behavior as suggested by Suedfeld (1979). Specific research efforts are discussed such as that of Greeley and McCready (1975) on the numbers of people involved in mystical experiences, Budzynski's (1979) work on suspending the critical left involvement, and La Berge's (1987) and Singer's (1966) work on dreaming. Research efforts on meditation are also examined, highlighting the techniques of Court (1984). In addition, specific research efforts in business are covered and Mihalsky (1974), Agor (1985) and Jung's (1979) ideas on building bridges from the Conscious to the Unconscious are explored.

Last of all this chapter considers specific tests and instruments that have been developed to assess intuition such as those of Ahsen (1972), Shorr (1982), Agor (1985) and Goldberg (1983).

The Intuitive Experience as Flow

Csikszentmihalyi (1979) conceptualizes heightened awareness as "the flow." He states that the clearest sign of flow is the experience of merging action and awareness. When a person is "in flow," they do not operate with the normal dualistic perspective. They are aware of their actions, but not of the awareness itself. The moment the awareness is split, in order to perceive, the flow is interrupted.

According to Csikszentmihalyi, people can maintain a short period of what he calls *merged awareness*. Merging of action and awareness is accomplished through a centering of attention, or centering on a limited stimulus field. Conscious effort is used to keep potentially intruding stimuli out of attention.

Maslow (1971) spoke of the flow as a narrowing of consciousness, a giving up of the past and the future.

In training sessions, we asked individuals to share these moments of flow. They described the flow experience as a feeling of fusion with the world. One poet described it as being in a state of ecstacy ... "my hand seems devoid of myself ... I just sat there watching in a state of awe and wonderment. And it just flows out by itself."

Spearman's Three Principles of Cognition

In order to more fully understand the inner way of knowing, we revisited Spearman's three principles of cognition. The first principle is that a man can know his own experiences as items of thought or, more formally, items of cognition. Having had an experience, a man can know that he has had such an experience. The second principle of cognition is that, given two items of cognition, it is possible for a man to conceive or invent relationships between them. It is in this second principle that we see inventions. The third principle is that with an item of cognition, plus a relationship, man can invent another item fulfilling the same relationship.

When any item of cognition and the relation to it is presented to the mind, the mind can then generate another related item. The degree of creativeness is the utmost to which the human mind can attain under any condition. Being inventive helps unlock doors to new knowledge. By training intuition, our consciousness can be described as a process called "looking out through a private door." Suedfeld suggests a unique way of understanding this process.

Mystical and Intuitive Experiences as Adaptive Behavior

Suedfeld (1979) reports on a promising conceptual approach to understanding mystical and intuitive experiences. It is called conceptualizing the human being as an organism that needs a constant flow of information to guide behavior. Suedfeld hypothesizes that, in a novel situation, or one that is dangerous or isolated, the individual will attend to and elaborate more on residual stimuli. His suggestion is that the mystical and intuitive experience is an adaptive reaction, or a frantic search for stimulation and information.

Another way to explore intuitive experiences was suggested by Simon Court in his book *Manual for Mediators*. He gave a list of words, synonyms or short phrases with dual meanings: one had a meaning with social significance, and another had a meaning that is physical or literal. His list included:

fire	bear	yield	strike	view
exhaust	taste	resolution	push	drag

According to Court, participants who have a relatively huge proportion of social associations tend to be emotionally dependent on their social environment. He ventures the hypothesis that inventive talent is more likely to score low on social associations of the words with dual meanings.

While the researcher or scientist can never see the subjects' actual inner imagery, any more than see an electron, it is possible to systematically employ scientific physiological or reporting measures to research and understand intuition. Abraham Maslow (1979) spoke of a fear of knowing; he said that this fear is also a fear *of doing* because of the responsibility inherent in new knowledge. Yet new knowledge often fits in well with our deeply buried knowledge. This dilemma was expressed by Marilyn Ferguson, who stated that it takes at least 50 years before a major scientific discovery penetrates the public consciousness; yet we need research to discover more about the nature, mechanisms and scope of these inner abilities.

Are We a Nation of Mystics?

In a 1979 *New York Times* magazine article ("Are We A Nation of Mystics?"), Andrew Greeley and William McReady pondered the propriety of approaching someone and asking, "Do you ever have religious mystic experiences?" In their actual work process, they found that, on pretests, 50% of their respondents reported having had mystical experiences; 45% stated experiencing feelings of being one with God and the universe.

In their national sample survey, Greeley and McCready attempted to fathom the unfathomable. They found that the relationship between frequent ecstatic experiences and psychological well-being was .40. Well-being was measured by using the Psychological Well-Being Scale developed by Norman Bradburn. The following common descriptors and percentages were tabulated:

Mystical Description	Percent Reported
A feeling of deep and profound peace	55
A certainty that all things would work out for the good	48
A sense of my own need to contribute to others	43
A conviction that love is at the center of everything	43
A sense of joy and laughter	43
A great increase in my understanding and knowledge	32

Suspending the Critical Left Involvement

Budzynski (1979) has worked with biofeedback to suspend the critical screening of the brain's left hemisphere. His simple technique overloads the brain with a meaningless task, such as repeating aloud a fast sequence of previously-recorded random numbers. From this exercise, the participants reported that it is impossible to consciously hear another tape recorded message being played at the same time.

By being completely self-conscious, man functions as a rational and wise individual. However, if we can discover ways to more often quiet the brain's left side, according to Budzynski, we can deepen our self-knowledge.

Dreaming as a Creative Process

According to researcher La Berge (1987) at Stanford University, dreaming is a creative process. In dreams, we accept what is there even though it may be repugnant or frightening. This attention differs from what we attend to while awake. When we are awake, our attention is selective and purposeful. La Berge has developed a tape-recorded process that teaches you how to induce lucid dreams, in which the dreamer wakes up and, while still inside the dream, consciously controls it.

Jerome Singer, a Yale University psychologist, has researched daydreaming. Singer (1966) states that the practiced daydreamer can learn the art of pacing so he/she can shift between inner and outer channels. By learning this shifting, the dreamer can heighten self-awareness and bring to consciousness many thoughts that lie dormant. To daydream, you must withdraw part of your attention from the environment. One way to withdraw attention, according to Singer, is to fix your gaze on a stationary object, such as a mandala. Try your ability to focus on this mandala.

Reproduced from *The Right-Brain Experience* by Marilee Zdenek. Copyright© 1983 by M. Zdenek. Reprinted by permission of McGraw-Hill Book Company, publishers.

From a series of experiments that examined the fantasy process, Singer (1966) concluded that there are distinct values to daydreaming. He reported that the participants unearthed a wealth of material. The subjects in Singer's study were seated in a small, dark sensory reduction chamber. They were asked to note their thought material every 15 seconds. Their reports were filled with fantasy.

In another experiment, a group was separated into two categories: high daydreamers and low daydreamers. Then both groups were colorfully insulted by the experimenter. Following these insults, the angry subjects were asked to tell Thematic Apperception Test Stories or to share their fantasy. Fantasy and daydreaming worked well in reducing anger; it worked best for those who were inclined to daydream.

Two other dream researchers, Agnew and Webb, reported in their book *Sleep and Dreams* (1975) that 50% of experimental research has concentrated on the dream cycle. There are four types of dreams: prophetic, interpretive, psychodynamic and biophysical. Prophetic dreams predict the future; interpretive dreams help us learn about an individual's true character; psychodynamics represent a safety valve to permit expression of thoughts and to get rid of psychic tensions; and, finally, biophysiological dreams can be divided into two different physiological patterns (REM and Non REM), and into neurological circuits with a biochemical basis.

Meditation

Meditation is a method of allowing consciousness to come through the private door. A helpful tool in using meditation is the *Meditators Manual*, published in 1984 by Simon Court. Court suggests that you conduct a conscious relaxing exercise, such as those suggested in Chapter Three. In the resulting state of relaxation, retain your mental concentration and ponder your reasons for wanting to meditate. You

Date	My Reasons for Meditating	
My Reasons for Meditating	This Will Show I Have Attained It	This Will Show I Have Failed to Attain It
1. _____	1. _____	1. _____
2. _____	2. _____	2. _____
3. _____	3. _____	3. _____

can then mentally note what the reasons are and continue to probe to allow as many reasons as possible to surface. After each session, write down your reasons. Court (1984) suggests the format on the preceding page.

In a recent workshop where participants discussed meditation, they reported the following reasons for meditating:
- to find out more about myself
- to gain self-knowledge
- to allow me to see things as they really are
- to withdraw into myself
- to seek guidance from within

The last reason recalls a very appropriate Dutch proverb. The proverb, shared by our friend Peter Spann from the Institute on Creativity in the Netherlands, reads: To change the world, you must start with yourself. To accomplish this, we should learn to see connections between what is inside and what is outside of ourselves, and how these two consciousnesses influence one another.

Why Meditate?

In examining the motives behind the need to practice some form of meditation, we usually find a desire for self-knowledge and self-fulfillment. Through meditation, individuals can become increasingly more aware of the world around them and of their own responsibility for what they experience. As we acknowledge circumstances that come and go as results of aspects of our own selves, we realize that the key to change is within ourselves. Consequently, if we modify our existence, we can bring into one accord our cherished values and ideals. This is not an easy task. It requires vigilance.

Intuition in Business

Douglas Dean and John Mihalsky are two pioneers who have impacted business in the understanding and use of intuition. A parapsychologist and an engineer (respectively), they tested the precognitive power of CEOs. They then studied the correlation between this ability and the profitability of each company. They asked the CEOs to predict a 100-digit number that was randomly selected by computer from two hours to two years later. They found that 80% of the CEOs who had doubled their company's profit within a five-year period had above average precognitive powers. The high scorers were described as dynamic and hurry-up bosses. The low scorers had a "mañana" attitude.

Mihalsky (1979) described precognition as a flow of information particles that move forward and backward in time. Information can be conceived as a continuum of matter and time. If information is approached from this vantage point, according to Mihalsky, it is continually available.

A problem that Mihalsky identified was how intuitive people responded to dominance. He found that an intuitive decision-maker will score poorly in precognitive tests if controlled by someone else.

Agor, a University of Texas professor, shared his research at a 1985 Key West seminar on Whole Brain Learning, in which he worked with over 2000 managers. In his national survey, Agor used a test composed of 27 multiple choice items based on the Myers-Briggs Type Indicator, which measures personality differences as well as intuitive ability. He found that top level managers relied on intuition.

Building Bridges from Conscious to Unconscious

Many activities build bridges from the conscious to the unconscious. Carl Jung spent most of his life devoting himself to inner experiences and attempted to form a unity with inner experiences and external phenomena. In Jung's therapy, Active Imagination, he counseled that you can cure a neurosis by building bridges between conscious and unconscious behavior. He reports on a patient whom he instructed to create; inasmuch as she could overcome her difficulties in her imagination, she could overcome them in her psyche. And she did. She found meaning in the visible as well as the hidden.

Jung used mandalas as a technique in making bridges between his conscious and unconscious. Every morning, he sketched a mandala which seemed to correspond to his inner situation at the time. In working with mandalas, Jung said that all its paths seemed to lead back to a single point, namely the midpoint. (See the mandala in this chapter.)

Remember: if you understand and experience the bridge in this life, you will have a link with the infinite desires; then, change can occur.

Some specific ideas and techniques on building bridges by meditation are suggested by Court (1984):

- Close your eyes and relax
- Count one for each breath you take in
- Count one for each breath you breathe out

Try to have no thoughts during the exercise, but do not be concerned about thoughts that do come to your mind.

Most people can count to 20 without any images flowing through their mind. Counting to 50 without images is quite an achievement. Participants who try this technique report that suddenly their minds go blank, images come and thoughts begin rushing through their minds. Others report a steady stream of thoughts, occasionally experiencing the ability to think and count at the same time. The breathing technique brings the outside world into us. When we close our eyes and withdraw our senses from the world around us, we enter another realm. Here we can ponder our future, muse over the past, daydream and play out fantasies. Court suggests other helpful activities such as seed thought and sound pondering.

Activity: Seed Thought

In Seed Thought, you begin with a thought and proceed to ponder it. This attracts an associated thought and then you ponder upon the new thought. This attracts yet another associated thought or idea; you mentally note each thought and continue to build a chain of linked ideas. An example of a seed thought: The wise seek everything within; the ignorant from without.

Activity: Sound Pondering

Another activity to try is to ponder sounds. You might want to listen to a mantra or a nadam. First, relax and give yourself over to the sound. Mentally note any thoughts or feelings that can be captured, and record them later in a journal.

One useful mantra is OM (rhymes with home) or Om Nama Shivaya. Nadams that you might want to try are a waterfall or a roaring ocean. Whatever you use should involve a continuous sound to allow you to use your imagination.

Tests to Assess Intuition or Inner Knowing

Ahsen Age Projection Test

The age projection test as developed by psychiatrist Akhter Ahsen (1972) uses imagery and the inner way of knowing as a tool for self-understanding. First, the therapist asks the client to give his first name and any nicknames that might have been given to him, particularly in childhood. Then the therapist interacts with the client by repeating certain descriptive words over and over. These words are salient descriptiors or features of symptoms that have been reported in former counseling sessions or gathered from the case history. These descriptors are addressed to the various names of the client such as, "Nickie, you're such an irresponsible boy!" or "Nicholas, we are letting you go because of your lack of responsibility."

The repetition of the descriptors activates the symptom and this in turn activates self-imagery. As the client experiences the images, he is asked to share the self-image, the place where it happened and the events that occurred during the age projected in the image. Lastly, the client is encouraged to share the events that occurred during the year prior to the age projected.

As the client and the therapist focus on neglected aspects of the patient's experience, release and self-knowledge come from the suppressed responses and lead to a catharsis of accumulated affect (Ahsen, 1972).

Eidetic Parents Test (EPT)

In the Eidetic Parents Test developed by Ahsen (1972), the client is asked to picture his parents in the house where they lived for the longest time, the house that gives them a feeling of home. Then certain questions are asked:

Where do you see your parents?
What are they doing?
How do you feel when you see these images?

As the client experiences the images and answers the questions, insight and release take place first by sharpening and strengthening the images, and later through discussion with the therapist.

Ahsen states that any reaction or memory that is communicated with the pictures he calls eidetic images, which are steppingstones to higher consciousness.

Shorr Imagery Test (SIT)

The SIT is a projective test that uses imagery and yields both a quantitative conflict score and a qualitative personality analysis. The SIT was developed by Shorr (1982) in his Los Angeles clinic in 1976. Shorr's work uses imagery as a method of self-observation in therapy, and he has been instrumental in the work of the Association for the Study of Mental Imagery.

Agor Intuitive Scale

Agor's (1984) test or scale is based on the Myers-Briggs Type Indicator.

The questions deal with problem solving preferences, thinking styles, learning styles, receptivity to new ideas, and interacting with others.

Agor found that top-level managers are intuitive, and that Asians scored higher than Occidentals. In a follow-up study of the top intuitive managers, Agor asked for examples of specific decisions they had made based primarily on intuition. All but one of the 70 in the follow-up study reported using intuition in making important decisions. Agor describes their actions as a subconscious harmony drawn from innumerable stored experiences. It also appeared that intuition worked best when the situation involved was high-risk and where there was little precedent.

Goldberg's Test on Intuitive Powers

Goldberg (1983) in his book *The Intuitive Edge* shares a 32-item test that yields an indication of one's ability to use intuition-enhancing behavior. The scale and scoring are as follows:

Intuitive Powers

1. When I don't have a ready answer, I tend to be:
   A. patient
   B. uneasy

2. When faced with uncertainty, I usually:
   A. become disoriented
   B. remain comfortable

3. In challenging situations, I am highly motivated and deeply committed:
   A. most of the time
   B. infrequently

4. When my intuition differs from the facts, I usually:
   A. trust my feelings
   B. follow the logical course

5. When working on a difficult problem, I tend to:
   A. concentrate on finding the solution
   B. play around with possibilities

6. When I disagree with others, I tend to:
   A. let them know about it
   B. keep the disagreement to myself

7. Generally speaking, I:
   A. prefer the same way
   B. enjoy taking risks

8. When working on a problem I change strategies:
   A. seldom
   B. often

9. I prefer to be told:
   A. exactly how to do things
   B. only what needs to be done

10. When things get very complicated, I:
    A. become exhilarated
    B. become insecure

11. When faced with a problem, I usually:
    A. create a plan or outline before getting started
    B. plunge right in

12. In most cases:
    A. change makes me nervous
    B. I welcome unexpected changes

13. My reading consists of:
    A. a variety of subjects, including fiction
    B. factual material mainly related to my work

14. When my opinion differs from the experts, I usually:
    A. stick to my belief
    B. defer to authority

15. When faced with a number of tasks, I:
    A. tackle them simultaneously
    B. finish one before going on to another

16. When learning something new, I:
    A. master the rules and procedures first
    B. get started and learn the rules as I go along

17. At work I prefer to:
    A. follow a prearranged schedule
    B. make my own schedule

18. At school I was (am) better at:
    A. essay questions
    B. short-answer questions

19. Basically, I am:
    A. an idealist
    B. a realist

20. When I make a mistake, I tend to:
    A. second-guess myself
    B. forget it and go on

21. The following statement best applies to me:
    A. I can usually explain exactly why I know something
    B. often I can't describe why I know something

22. When offering a description or explanation, I am more likely to rely on:
    A. analogy and anecdote
    B. facts and figures

23. I can usually be convinced by:
    A. an appeal to reason
    B. an appeal to my emotions

24. When I am wrong, I:
    A. readily admit it
    B. defend myself

25. I would rather be called:
    A. imaginative
    B. practical

26. When faced with a difficult problem, I am likely to:
   A. ask for advice
   B. tackle it myself

27. Unpredictable people are:
   A. annoying
   B. interesting

28. When setting an appointment for the following week, I am likely to say:
   A. "Let's set an exact time now."
   B. "Call me the day before."

29. When something spoils my plans, I:
   A. get upset
   B. calmly make a new plan

30. When I have a hunch, I usually react with:
   A. enthusiasm
   B. mistrust

31. Most of my friends and colleagues:
   A. believe in the value of intuition
   B. are skeptical about intuition

32. I am best known as:
   A. an idea person
   B. a detail person

Scoring

Give yourself one point if you answered A on the following items: 1, 3, 4, 6, 10, 13, 14, 15, 18, 19, 22, 24, 25, 30, 31, 32.

Score one point if you answered B on the following items: 2, 5, 7, 8, 9, 11, 12, 16, 17, 20, 21, 23, 26, 27, 28, 29.

If your total score is 24 or above, you tend strongly toward an intuitive approach to decisions and problems. More than likely you trust your intuition, as well you should, since it is probably highly accurate.

If your total is between 16 and 23, you tend to vary in style but are more intuitive than analytic or systematic. Your intuition is probably correct more often than not.

If your total is between 8 and 15, you tend to mix styles but lean more toward the analytic and rational than the intuitive. Your intuition might be erratic.

If your total is below 8, you lean heavily toward a systematic-rational approach to problems and decisions. Chances are you do not trust your intuition very much, perhaps because of past experiences when it has been wrong.

In evaluating these results, do not regard this test as a definitive measure of your intuitive capacity. For one thing, there are no universally accepted standards for making such judgments; and there has been no systematic attempt to determine either intuitive ability or style. And furthermore the tests have not been validated with long-term use.

Goldberg makes this important point: you are likely to be more intuitive and to trust your intuition more in some situations than others. A high score on the questionnaire is a good indication of positive, intuitive-enhancing behavior. In that respect, the questions can also serve as a tool for introspection and improvement.

Research on understanding and assessing intuition is a dynamic field of study, and involves researchers and practitioners from many disciplines. Some other notables include Jonas Salk who has dedicated himself to exploring inner knowing and Karl Pribham, a neuroscientist who coined the term "feed forward." Feed forward describes those images that spur us on to creative action. The research suggests that confidence and belief in the process is one of the chief allies in the effectiveness of the use of intuition.

References

Agnew, H. & Webb, W. (1973). *Sleep and dreams.* IA: William C. Brown.
Agor, W. H. (1984). *Intuitive management: Integrating left and right management skills.* Englewood Cliffs, NJ: Prentice-Hall.
Ahsen, A. (1968). *Basic concepts in eidetic psychotherapy.* NY: Brandon House.
Ahsen, A. (1972). *Eidetic parents test and analysis.* NY: Brandon House.
Ahsen, A. (1977). *Psych-eye.* NY: Brandon House.
Brunton, P. (1935). *The secret path.* NY: E. P. Dutton.
Budzynski, T. (1979). Biofeedback and the thought stages of consciousness. In D. Goleman & R. Davidson (Eds.), *Consciousness: Brain, states of awareness and mysticism.* NY: Harper & Row.
Court, S. (1984). *Meditators manual.* London, England: Aquarius Press.
Csikszentmihalyi M. (1979). The flow experience in consciousness. In D. Goleman & R. Davidson (Eds.), *Consciousness: Brain, states of awareness and mysticism.* NY: Harper & Row.

Goldberg, P. (1983). *The intuitive edge.* Los Angeles, CA: Jeremy P. Tarcher, Inc.
Goldfried, M. (1971). Systematic desensitization as training in self control. *Journal of Consulting and Clinical Psychology, 37* (2), 228-234.
Greeley, A. & McCready, W. (1979). Are we a nation of mystics? *NY: Times Magazine.*
Jung, C. G. (1979). *Words and images.* Princeton, NJ: Bollingen Services, Princeton University Press.
La Berge, S. (1987). *Awake in your sleep.* Los Angeles, CA: Jeremy P. Tarcher, Inc.
Mahoney, M. (1974). *Cognition and behavior modification.* Cambridge, MA: Bollingen Press.
Maslow, A. (1971). *The farther reaches of human nature.* NY: Viking Press.
Mihalsky, J. (1979). Executive ESP. In D. Goleman & R. Davidson (Eds.), *Consciousness: Brain, states of awareness and mysticism.* NY: Harper & Row.
Myers, I. B. (1976). *Myers-Briggs type indicator.* Palo Alto, CA: Consulting Psychologists Press.
Shorr, J. (1982). Discoveries about the mind's ability to organize and find meaning in imagery. In J. Shorr, G. Sobel, P. Robin & J. Cannella (Eds.), *Imagery: Its many dimensions and applications:* NY: Plenum Press.
Singer, J. (1966). *Daydreaming.* NY: Random House.
Spearman, C. (1904). General intelligence - Objectivity determined and measured. *American Journal of Psychology, 15* (1), 207-293.
Suedfeld, P. (1979). A case for interdisciplinary research. In D. Goleman & R. Davidson (Eds.), *Consciousness: Brain, states of awareness and mysticism.* NY: Harper & Row.
Zdenek, M. (1983). *The right brain experience.* NY: McGraw Hill.

CHAPTER THREE

Developing and Increasing Intuition

*Again and again,
Step by step,
Intuition opens the doors
That lead to man's
designing
Of more advantageous
rearrangements.*

Buckminster Fuller
Intuition

Intuition does not come to us on demand. We have to be prepared for it, yet there are several methods that can help encourage intuition. Attitude is part of the basic process of encouraging intuition as well as one's behavior and to truly tap the powers of the intuitive, we must create an appropriate personal climate for intuition to develop or emerge. Skepticism of intuitive powers is negative programming. So is feeling that discussing intuition and its nurturance is slightly alchemy-oriented. Negative programming makes it very difficult to tap into intuition. On the other hand, approaching situations that are uncertain and where facts and reason may not appear, in a positive manner encourages and stimulates intuition.

Number one on the list of ways to stimulate intuition is to not take yourself so seriously and to program some play into your life. Second, adopt an attitude of relaxed *decision-making* and *problem-solving* and allow some problems to be solved in a non-linear fashion. Ashley Montagu defined over-reliance on the linear as analytical thinking psychosclerosis, or a type of mental rigidity which stifles intuition. A rigid mind has a tendency to reject intuition while a flexible mind, or one that is conceptually open, is willing to relinquish control and predictability for the pay-off of providing the intuitive mind with opportunities to emerge.

There are a number of ways to encourage intuition: formulating problems that can be presented to the unconscious, setting goals, using affirmations to create a climate for positive thinking and the emergence of intuition, using dreams as a source of intuition, meditation, relaxation and autogenic training. We will explore these, as well as physical activity to quiet the mind, examples of conditions for intuition and imaging techniques that relate to the development of intuition. Before engaging in the suggested activities in this chapter, we suggest you identify enthusiasm within yourself for the exploration. The Latin derivative for enthusiasm is *en theos* or *God within*. It is our intent that through this exploration you will become better acquainted with your inner (or higher) self and be able to invite that self in at will.

Formulating Problems

The problem-solving ability of the mind is remarkable. A suitable metaphor for the brain is the computer: with the correct input, the brain "programs" the unconscious. Like a mathematical formula, input plus processing time equals output. Think of an unconscious idea-processor waiting for you to provide input. What problem do you want to assign to it? Identify the problem that you want to explore and write a brief paragraph describing it.

As you write, be very clear. The more precise you are, the more accurate your unconscious can be. Also, be complete and try to include all details. Invest the problem with intent or strength, and let your unconscious know that this is a serious problem. With these suggestions in mind, now rewrite your problem in as clear, complete and strong a manner as possible.

Read your problem to yourself, relax your body and mind and visualize the problem. Allow images to flow and invite your unconscious to solve the problem. Some answers will simply present themselves, while others may require a period of incubation. You may need to sleep on it, place the problem on the back burner or – to use the computer metaphor – go off-line. At this time, it might be helpful to do some relaxation activities, to daydream, meditate, or fall asleep while your personal computer processes the problem.

When you receive an answer, it may be as sudden as a flash of lightning or in a Eureka type revelation. Describing this moment, many people say it is as if the answer or inspiration comes from somewhere or something else, not from themselves.

Another way to formulate problems and seek clarity and completeness is to construct a type of mapping called *futures wheel of the problem*. This technique, developed by futurist Jerry Glenn from Washington, DC, would look like the following figure:

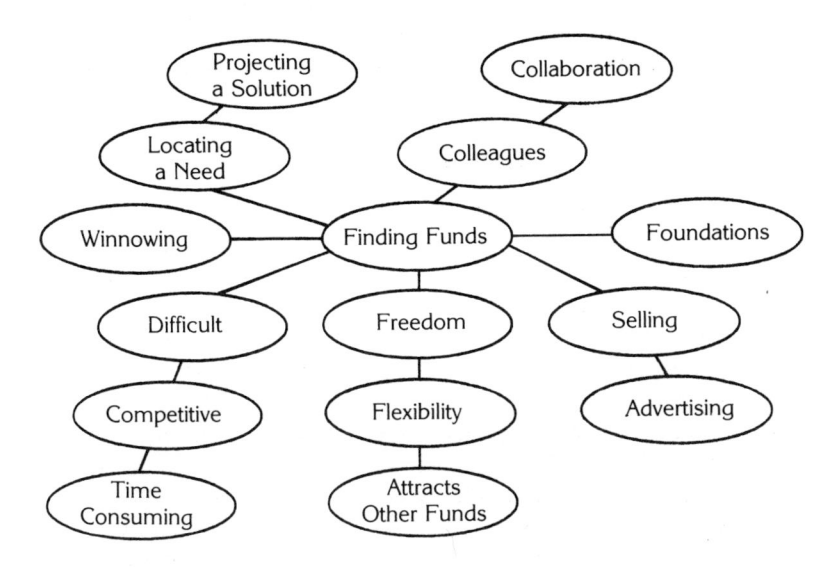

```
        Projecting              Collaboration
        a Solution
    Locating              Colleagues
    a Need
Winnowing          Finding Funds           Foundations
    Difficult              Freedom              Selling
    Competitive            Flexibility          Advertising
    Time                   Attracts
    Consuming              Other Funds
```

The individual who constructed this figure used a futures wheel to explore the problem of finding funds, and was able to clarify the need for addressing a real problem or locating a need. She chose the equity issue in minority education, and examined what the funding would provide, such as freedom and flexibility. The examination process gave strength to the problem. In identifying the negative points of fundraising, she became aware of its time-consuming nature, and that it is a difficult and competitive process. She viewed the two poles of positive impact and negative forces as a process of winnowing. Lastly, she explored ways in which she might collaborate with colleagues, or identify who shared her interest in such a project. In what ways might they work together to secure what they all wanted? What they wanted was to impact minority education. The funds became the vehicle. Through such simple exploration of ideas, deferring evaluation or analysis, her thoughts and feelings concerning a situation were identified in a variety of ways.

Once the question is formulated, it can then be offered to the unconscious. Carl Jung (1964) suggests that your answer may be presented by the intuitive mind through synchronicity. Synchronicity consists of coincidences that are not causally related, but that contain substantive meaning. He suggests that some undiscovered interaction happens between the environment, the unconscious and the conscious mind. In a sense, the intuitive mind resonates with a pattern of information waves and then quietly points out or directs action that appears to be random behavior.

Establishing Goals

Sometimes we cannot engage our intuition in helping us reach our goals because our goals are not clear. Yet when we have a clear, strong goal with a strong intention, we can become goal driven. It is almost as though someone is shining a light in a tunnel and saying, "Here I am." Discovering what we want in life can be facilitated through the process of setting goals. Setting goals facilitates a more harmonious flow through life; that is, if you believe that the nature of life is movement, change and creativity, then goals can help to provide a clear focus and direction. To illustrate this phenomenon, begin by examining several broad categories. For example, do you want to make changes or establish goals in your relationships, your career, leisure time, life style, personal growth or some other category? Write this area down on a blank sheet of paper.

Another activity to help clarify your values and attitudes is this: Draw a triangle and, at each corner, identify a wish for "my self," for "my country" and for "my world."

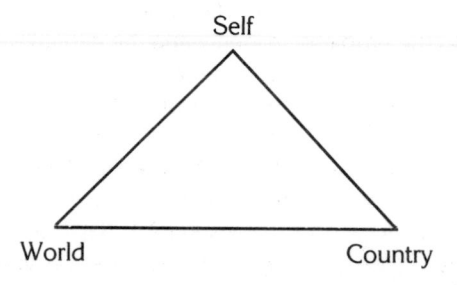

```
              Self
              /\
             /  \
            /    \
           /      \
          /_____\
       World      Country
```

This exercise stretches you to think beyond the present situation. If you are working in a group, after each person completes a triangle, the group can share the images. Sharing invests both strength and intention in the wishes.

If you are working by yourself, think of all the changes you might want in your life, in your country, in your world. Some people want world peace, the end of poverty, communication amongst all peoples, family-type schools and people experiencing love. Remember, you can be as creative as you want in this exercise. Create a mental picture of your dreams or wishes for the world, your country, yourself.

Now, select goals for one year. Write the goals as if they have been achieved. Some goals might be:

- I own 150 acres of prime farm land with a beautiful farm house, horses, and a river running through the property. I raise horses. I support myself easily and successfully.

- I sing my own songs in a fashionable restaurant and hotel. The songs have been released on a new recording. I am often recognized in public and people ask for my autograph.

- I have written a book on Creativity that has sold over 600,000 copies. It is being syndicated on TV for a talk show. I will be the host on the program.

Now write your five-year goals, and make sure that they are in agreement with your one-year goals. Goals can interact and complement one another.

Now write out your goals for six months, one month and even for one week.

In goal-setting workshops, we usually provide notebooks and encourage the participants to use different colored pencils, to date the work and to examine their goals frequently, revising and reshaping wherever necessary.

Some general recommendations for goal setting:

1. *Strive for realism.* Identify short-term goals that you can accomplish. However, to stretch your sights, your long-range goals can be wonderfully expansive and imaginative.
2. *When you fail to achieve a goal, decide if you want to set it again or let it go.* And when you accomplish a goal, give yourself recognition and a reward.
3. *Don't take on more than you can accomplish.* Simplify. Choose goals that you truly like and desire.

The Use of Affirmations to Create a Climate of Positive Thinking

Maxwell Maltz (1960) in *Psychocybernetics* suggests that affirmations are used every day of our lives and that often these affirmations are negative. When we experience anxiety, inadequacy or humiliation under the guise of worry about performance, we are negatively affirming ourselves with a feeling of success. Maltz suggests that when we define a goal, we picture having achieved it. See that picture clearly and vividly and be aware of the feelings that surround the accomplishment of the goal.

Athletic coaches use affirmations by encouraging athletes to visualize themselves performing and being successful and better than other athletes. Some affirmations that were generated in a recent leadership training institute are:

I am totally healthy and effective in my life.
I am loving and responsive to my family.
My intuitive mind is helping me solve my problems.
I am confident and capable.
I am capable of love for myself and others.
I have respect and regard for myself and others.
I am a lovable and likable person.
I am successful in my personal and professional life.
I am achieving my life goals.

The more specific the affirmation, the more the intuitive mind can help you make a breakthrough. Make your own list of affirmations and repeat them several times a day.

A set of affirmations that was suggested by Harman and Rheingold (1984) in their book *Higher Creativity: Liberating the Unconscious for Breakthrough Insights* is:

I am not separate.
I can trust.
I can know.
I am responsible.
I am single-minded.

They suggest that you simply affirm these several times a day for a period of six months and imagine the full meaning of each statement. We have tried this exercise in leadership training and the results are amazing. People state that it helps free them to be more creative, to feel more positive about themselves and to feel more integrated. Robert

Browning expressed the value of affirmations in his poem *Paracelsus* ... "truth is within ourselves ... "

The Use of Dreams as a Source of Intuition

Solutions to problems and creative breakthroughs often come in dream form. The poet Coleridge awakened from a dream and wrote the poem *Kubla Khan*. Rene Descartes, a young soldier, realized in a dream that he should combine mathematics and philosophy into a new discipline. The scientist Kekule's dancing snakes and his dream-inspired notion of the benzene ring is yet another example of using dreams as a source of intuition.

Recurring dreams can be a source of intuitive messages. Keep a note pad and a pen beside your bed. Upon awakening, jot down your dreams, then, begin to note the patterns that evolve. A problem with dreams is that they are symbolic and need interpretation. To harness dreams to build your intuition, suggest to yourself before going to sleep that *you will* dream certain aspects of a dream and that *you will* remember them.

Lucid dreaming is learning to act with the dream ego. In lucid dreaming, dream figures are confronted and the direction or pattern of the dream is changed; you become the director. Stephen La Berge (1981) has worked on the study of lucid dreaming at the Sleep Research Center of the Stanford University School of Medicine. La Berge taught his participants to have lucid dreams at will and to communicate to outside observers from within their dreams. These dreamers were then led to explore the nature of the dream state. La Berge monitored respiration, pulse, brain waves, muscle activity and eye movements. He found he could use these physiological measures to signal to observers that the patient was dreaming. La Berge states that in the dream state you can act intentionally and actively intervene. La Berge calls his five step procedure MILD (Mnemonic Induction of Lucid Dreams):

1. Awaken spontaneously from a dream in the morning.
2. After memorizing the dream, engage in ten to fifteen minutes of reading or any other activity demanding full wakefulness.
3. Then while lying in bed and returning to sleep, say, "Next time I'm dreaming, I want to remember I'm dreaming."
4. Visualize your body asleep in bed with rapid eye movements; at the same time, see yourself in the dream you just rehearsed and realize that you are in fact dreaming.

5. Repeat steps three and four until you feel your intention is clearly fixed.

La Berge hypothesizes that the waking state and sleeping state can be combined. He suggests that lucid dreaming can be to dreaming what enhanced waking consciousness can be to consciousness – a state in which one consciously creates reality.

Meditation as a Source of Intuition

Meditation, if practiced routinely, is an effective technique for expanding consciousness. Most meditators recommend two twenty minute sessions a day to allow your mind to become quiet and clear. Effective meditation is natural and effortless. Some meditation techniques require concentration or focusing on a single object, idea or concept to keep your attention from wandering and serve to blank the mind. However, too much effort can cause mental strain and render meditation useless.

A friend of ours recently said that he had lost his sense of freedom over the last five years. Then while meditating one afternoon, he experienced the same wonderfully exuberant feeling he had known before. Since then, daily silent meditation has retained a prominent place in his life. His feeling of lifting up has restored his lost sense of freedom.

Simple relaxation procedures and visualizations of being on a secluded beach or in a special place can provide positive vehicles for meditation.

Relaxation Invites Intuition

When your body and mind are deeply relaxed, your brain wave patterns change and become slower. This deeper, slower pattern is called the alpha level, a healthful state of consciousness because of its relaxing effect on the mind and body. If you already have your own method of relaxing deeply or going into a quiet meditative state, continue to use it. If you do not have a relaxation method, you may want to follow these directions:

Get in a comfortable position, either sitting or lying down, and in a quiet place where you will not be disturbed. Relax your body completely, beginning with your toes and work up to your head. Actively picture each muscle in your body being relaxed in turn. Let all of your tension flow out of your body. Breathe deeply and slowly from your abdomen. Count down slowly from 10 to 1, feeling yourself become more deeply relaxed with each count.

Deep relaxation is healthful and beneficial both mentally and physically, and helpful in preparing the intuitive self to emerge.

Autogenic Training

J. H. Schultz developed Autogenic Training, a process in which the patient learns to move through a series of body states that correspond to shifting states of consciousness (Schultz & Lutke, 1959). Self-hypnosis was monitored as the patients concentrated on making their hands feel warm and their limbs feel heavy. To get an idea of autogenic training, sit down, close your eyes and breathe deeply and relax for a few minutes. Then say softly to yourself, "my hands are warm, my arms are feeling heavy." By focusing on your body, you create a communication channel between the volition and relaxation states. Schultz found that achieving relaxation during waking hours is a form of self-education and that there is a close correlation between what people hold in their mind's eye and in what happens within their bodies.

Still another way to become aware of your body is to experience the difference between the relaxed and tense states in your body. Tightly clench your fist and then let it relax. Now systematically relax all muscle groups, moving progressively through your body. Start with your toes, work your way up to your legs, midsection, chest, arms, fingers, neck, face, and scalp. By doing this, you can achieve a deep relaxation in which your conscious is subdued and quieted and where that still, small voice from your unconscious can make itself known to you.

Physical Activity to Quiet the Mind and Invite Intuition

As you let your focus shift to physical activity, restful alertness can be achieved. Restful alertness has a positive intuition-enhancing effect which may or may not lead to an immediate intuitive breakthrough.

Yoga quiets the mind and decreases tension. As the body becomes more flexible, a number of exercises can be accomplished prior to meditation. One effective exercise is the back stretch. Sit on the floor with your legs straight ahead. Bend your body forward, slowly sliding your hands along the top of your legs. Grasp your toes. Without bending your knees, pull your torso a little lower toward your legs. Use your arms rather than your back muscles. Remember, this is a *gentle* exercise. Relax your whole body and hold for a count of ten seconds. This exercise can be repeated two or three times.

Another simple exercise is the shoulder stand. Lie flat on your back with your feet together and your arms at your sides. Brace your palms against the floor, stiffen your stomach and slowly raise your legs. Keep your knees straight. When your legs are perpendicular to the floor, swing them up so that your hips leave the floor. Brace your palms against your lower back for support. Hold this position for twenty to thirty seconds at first. Then gradually increase the time. These two positions are the type of stretching exercises that are helpful in quieting the mind.

In addition, the alternate tensing of the various muscles and letting them go has a calming effect. At work, you can quickly relax by concentrating on your face. Close your eyes and raise your eyebrows as high as possible. Hold this position for ten seconds and then allow your face to relax. Frown and lower your brows. Relax and repeat. Open your mouth as wide as possible. Hold, then relax. By doing this simple exercise you can relax and clear your head prior to situations where you want to have your intuitive mind's assistance.

Establishing Conditions for Intuition: Examples of Creative People

Knowlson (1980) in his book on *Originality: A Popular Study of the Creative Mind* collected examples of ways in which creative people invited intuition:

- Schiller used the scent of decomposing apples in his desk
- Proust wrote in a soundproof room
- Kipling needed jet black ink to write
- Kant wrote in bed at precise times of day, staring through the window at a tower
- Samuel Johnson used a purring cat, an orange peel and a cup of tea

Other examples from Hutchinson (1949) in *How to Think Creatively*:

- Rousseau thought bare-headed in full sunshine
- Beethoven poured cold water over his head to stimulate his brain
- Rossini covered himself with blankets while composing
- Dickens turned his bed to the north so that the magnetic forces could help him create

These are eccentricities, but they did work for these creative people.

Perhaps they worked because they had faith in them or because these idiosyncratic actions served as stimuli to trigger intuition.

Hutchinson lists a few helpful suggestions about the attitudes that underlie tapping into the intuitive:

- Increase your motivation by anticipating the satisfaction of achievement
- Increase your preparation by believing the problem is not an insoluble one for you
- Believe the answer will come, although you may have to wait or grow into it
- Realize that rest is essential when you feel defeated by a problem

Imaging Techniques as They Relate to Intuition

Imagery offers a clue to how society views the creative process. Western culture often equates creativity with imagination, for the ability to imagine or to conjure up images different from others is recognized as creative. Bronowski (1978), in the *Origins of Knowledge and Imagination,* states that the eye interprets the world through a process of inference. But just as the eye makes inferences about objects, so the brain tends to perceive ideas, concepts and feelings as being related, if their general characteristics seem familiar. In a recent issue of the *American Psychologist,* Roger Shepherd wrote that mental imagery is remarkably able to substitute for actual perception. He found that his subjects made the same judgments about objects in their absence as in their presence. Imagery can be called the language of the unconscious. The power of the unconscious is most directly evoked by the deliberate practice of imagery and visualization skills.

Communication between our conscious and unconscious works in two ways. Images are the messengers from the deeper mind to carry inspirations to surface awareness. Images are also used to transmit messages from the conscious mind to deeper parts of the unconscious. The following scenario is an example of imagery that can be helpful in the early stages of visualization training. The purpose of the image-journey is to open the mind's gate to the flow of images. It is meant to be a guide and a model, but not a strict prescription.

Imagine yourself reclining on a bed of soft fragrant grass on a gentle slope beneath a large tree. The air is warm and, with each breath, your lungs fill with fresh, clean air that is revitalizing. Pay attention to your breathing and with each breath feel yourself becoming lighter. Take a deep breath and see yourself floating effortlessly from the ground.

See yourself floating out over a meadow that leads to a mountainside. There are small goats below shepherded by a young boy. This scene causes you to smile because of its peacefulness. As you float toward the mountain, feel yourself slowly descending until you are standing on a trail in a wooded area. See yourself walking up the trail. Feel the cool green foliage as you pass and on your face the warmth of the sunlight filtering through the trees. Up and up you effortlessly climb until you come to the top of the hill. There on the summit is a wise old man who is sitting quietly beside a fire. He gestures to you to be seated and you do. What questions do you want to ask this wise old man? Ask him. Become the wise old man and see yourself sitting there expectantly waiting for an answer. What do you say to yourself?

The wise old man reaches into a leather pouch and takes out an object for you. Holding the object in your hand, slowly begin your trip back down the hillside. Fix the impressions from your journey in your consciousness.

See yourself reaching the bottom of the hill and beginning to float back to your beginning point. Count to three, open your eyes and reflect upon your journey.

The images that may have appeared on this guided imagery-trip can be important clues to your feelings and may represent solutions to current problems. Sometimes the meanings of the images, specifically the image of the gift, become clear later. Time may be necessary for full understanding.

Another effective visualization exercise is called The Three Gates which was developed by Joseph E. Shorr (1982), a psychologist who has developed a type of psycho-therapy he calls psycho-imagination therapy. The Three Gates activity is this:

Relax yourself and slowly imagine that you are standing in front of three gates in a row, one beyond the other. Take your time seeing yourself opening each one in turn. Then report what you see, do, and feel.

We have used a similar activity that involves three boxes. The individual participant is encouraged to describe the contents of a large, medium and small box. In a study entitled "Discoveries About the Mind's Ability to Organize and Find Meaning in Imagery," Shorr reported that about 90% of the persons participating in the imaginary situation saw the gates as progressing toward the deeper unconscious levels. Some went past the third gate to a fourth gate to reveal unconscious material.

The most important thing to remember is not to be discouraged if your first guided imagery journey is not spectacular. As you repeat exercises like this one, you learn the language of your unconscious and how to understand what it is communicating to you. Remember that imagery is the language of the unconscious, and the power of the unconscious is most directly evoked by the *deliberate* practice of imagery and visualization.

Specific Visualization Techniques to Stimulate Intuition

A favorite strategy that we have used in leadership workshops is called Buried Treasure. We provide lots of colored paper, crayons, chalk, felt-tip pens, a variety of magazines, books, cards, old photographs, stick-on letters and anything else that can be used to stimulate an artistic expression of the buried treasure that we all hold within. Then we begin with a relaxation exercise and some quiet meditation to enable the participants to visualize the desired reality. Participants are urged to see their goals as clearly as possible. They are asked to concentrate on the image and to focus energy on the scene. Then they are encouraged to create an actual picture of their buried treasure.

At a Whole Brain Symposium held in Key West, the participants created a group collàge or Buried Treasure. Each person shared the objects that they had brought to the conference and why. This helped to invest strength in the pictures, poems, feathers, and brochures. A facilitator created the group collage which represented group goals, attitudes and values. The collage and the process were quite powerful. Perhaps you wish to isolate a specific area to work on, for example your health, or perhaps you want to work on your relationships with others. If you construct a small collage, you can tuck it into your appointment book to remind you of your goals. In this manner, you are consciously sending messages to your unconscious to accomplish or realize the goal.

One individual created a collage of a very attractive young man, dressed in a suit, carrying a briefcase and walking away from a roomful of people toward an obviously expensive car. Others created collages of themselves signing copies of their new books for fellow colleagues or sailing on their new boat or painting their new homes.

Placing a written affirmation on your buried treasure adds a verbal commitment: "Here I am driving my new Porsche. I love it and I have lots of capital to maintain this life style"

A favorite of one of our participants was: "Here I am in Hawaii. I earn lots of money to take several vacations a year." The collage included a tall, tan, trim young woman who represented a secondary goal of the participant, to slim down and to be more content with her physical image.

A variation of buried treasure is *Prime Time* in which you do the following:

Think of one goal that you want to accomplish. It can be a short-term or a long-term goal, but one that you really want to attain. Now, write the goal as clearly as possible in one sentence. Such as: "I want to have my own private consultation business."

Then write about your Prime Time dream. Use the present tense, as if you have already accomplished your dream. Remember, supply as much detail as possible.

An example for the private consultation business Prime Time might be: "I am sitting in my large well-lit office, in a building with a view of the bay. My secretary is bringing me today's mail prior to my staff conference with our eight consultants. I am trying to acocmplish a great deal today because we are going on a six-month training session to five different countries to train over 500 individuals. I'm wearing a big smile of pride and pleasure."

After you have written your Prime Time, relax and continue to visualize and add more details. Silently add an affirmation. Keep the Prime Time statement near you and read it often, making additions or deletions as necessary. Several of our participants have told us that, to their great amazement, their goals were reached and many just as they had visualized them.

Accessing Both Sides

Ned Herrmann, chairman of the Whole Brain Corporation in Lake Lure, North Carolina, has devised a 120-question instrument for determining cerebral preference. The instrument yields a brain dominance profile which is used to understand differences in work style and to program for harmony in corporations and within individuals.

Herrmann has gone beyond the notion of right-brain/left-brain dichotomous thinking and added the limbic areas. He describes the cerebral left as rational, cognitive, quantitative, and dealing basically with facts. The limbic left is organized, sequential and procedural dealing mostly with structure and controls. Herrmann reports the cerebral right quadrant as being visual, conceptual, and simultaneous, it can be thought of as *open* in contrast to *controlled*. The limbic right is emotional, expressive, and interpersonal, and can be characterized by feelings rather than facts.

Herrmann reports that, in examining data from over 500,000 surveys, he can spot technical engineering types in cerebral left; administrative and bookkeeper types in limbic left; personnel-oriented humanistic people in limbic right; and innovators, entrepreneurs and visionaries in cerebral right. He suggests that the use of total whole brain functioning can be actualized. Conscious efforts to stimulate cerebral right behavior include visualization, meditation, and relaxation. On the opposite side, cerebral left stimulation would include setting goals and formulating problems.

Whenever possible, we have integrated the two types of thinking – logical and linear, conceptual and gestalt – in our training activities. The intuitive process encourages ideas within the unconscious mind to surface. As we reflect, deliberate, or conceptualize, unconsciousness is lost. Thought interferes. It is important to remember that the intuitive mind needs time to itself, and it will take time for intuitive ability to develop. In a sense, we are turning off to tune in.

> *The seed of mystery lies in muddy water.*
> *How can I perceive this mystery?*
> *Water becomes still through stillness.*
> *How can I become still?*
> *By flowing with the stream.*
> **Lao Tzu**

Ornstein, a research psychologist at the University of California, believes people can, by viewing geometric forms, train the brain's right hemisphere to build up the intuitive side of themselves. In a recent trip to Bulgaria, one co-author spoke with the Bulgarian scientist Lozanov, who is using art to stimulate visualization and creative thought. Visualization enables us to concentrate on internalized geometric forms and strengthens the brain's right hemisphere. Other methods for developing intuitive functions are learning crafts and paying attention to dreams. When the right hemisphere or intuitive mode is developed, it will free the body energies.

Another suggestion comes from Shakti Gawain (1983), a teacher and trainer in developing creativity and in using your mental energy to transform and improve your health, prosperity and relationships, she calls her activity *divesting oneself.* In divesting oneself, you write down negative attitudes you think about yourself, other people, relationships, the world and life. Then sit quietly examining the list. After a few moments, deliberate and vigorously tear up the list and throw the pieces away. This act symbolizes how small an amount of power is needed to allow negative attitudes in your life. An exercise we often use is to go through closets, drawers, basement, garage or desk, wherever you have years of accumulated stuff, and throw or give it away.

As your actual house or your emotional house is placed in order, through this vigorous cleaning and straightening, you stimulate a mental, emotional and psychic clearing. Gawain suggests that you repeat an affirmation while divesting: The more I outflow, the more space I create for good things to come to me, the more my intuitive self is developed and increased.

References

Bronowski, J. (1973). *The ascent of man.* Boston, MA: Little, Brown.
Bronowski, J. (1978). *Origins of knowledge and imagination.* New Haven, CT: Yale University Press.
Fuller, B. (1972). *Intuition.* NY: Doubleday.
Gawain, S. (1983). *Creative visualization.* NY: Bantam Books.
Harman, W. & Rheingold, H. (1984). *Liberating the unconscious for breakthrough insights.* Los Angeles, CA: Jeremy P. Tarcher, Inc.
Herrmann, N. (1988). *The creative brain.* Lake Lore, NC: Brain Books.
Hutchinson, E. (1949). *How to think creatively.* NY: Abingdon-Cohesberry.
Jung, C. G. (1964). *Man and his symbols.* Garden City, NY: Doubleday.
Knowlson, T. (1980). *Originality: A popular study of the creative mind.* Darby, PA: Arden Library.
LaBerge, S. (1981). Lucid dreaming: Directing the action as it happens. *Psychology Today,* January, 48.
LaBerge, S. (1984). *Awake in your sleep.* Los Angeles, CA: Jeremy P. Tarcher, Inc.
Maltz, M. (1960). *Psychocybernetics.* NY: Prentice Hall.
Ornstein, R. (1973). *The nature of human consciousness.* San Francisco, CA: W. H. Feldman & Co.
Schultz, J. H. & Luthe, W. (1959). *Autogenic training: A psychological approach to psychotherapy.* NY: Grune & Stratton.
Shepherd, R. (1978). The mental image. *American Psychologist, 33* (2), 123-137.
Shorr, J. (1982). Discoveries about the mind's ability to organize and find meaning in imagery. In *Imagery: Its many dimensions and applications.* NY: Plenum Press.

CHAPTER FOUR

Children and Intuition

And a little child shall lead them.

Old Testament

Intuitive functioning is natural in children. According to Joseph Chilton Pearce (1985) in *The Magical Child Matures,* strong intuitive abilities appear around age four and disappear for most people at about age seven. The period between the ages of four and seven is a very interesting time span in a child's life. Pearce reports that psychiatrist Gerald Jampolsky tells of the four- and five-year-old children who are brought to him by their parents. Why do the parents of these children seek the guidance of a psychologist? Because the children tell of experiences that we would call extrasensory! Jampolsky states that many children show telepathic and clairvoyant capacities at age four, but that such potential usually disappears around age seven. He also reports on a colleague who, in obtaining her doctorate in musicology, found that virtually all normal-hearing four-year-old children had perfect pitch, but almost all had lost it at around age seven. The reason for the loss seems to be lack of development and stabilization of such intuitive ability during its specific time for development. If no model is given to stimulate and stabilize the capacity, it atrophies.

Pearce states that the loss seems to occur at age seven, as the child's focus of awareness shifts away from the primary brain system in order to develop the new brain and mind. If intuition has not been developed by then, through proper modeling and guidance, the possibility for such action generally atrophies, as the weight of attention shifts to the new blueprint.

Jerome Bruner (1977), a psychologist from Yale, refers to the fruits of intuitive thinking as "educated guesses." He believes that encouraging intuitive thinking in children will bear later rewards in "educated guesses," in situations where an immediate right answer is lacking. This theory is supported by the concept that, without practice, the ability wanes.

Some interesting work in nurturing children's intuition was reported by Magdelene Lampert in the *Journal of Curriculum Studies* (1984). Lampert states that Jeanne Bamberger at the Massachusetts Institute of Technology trained a group of elementary school teachers to recognize what she called "intuitive knowledge" in their students. Each individual builds a store of this common sense sort of information from personal experimentation on the physical environment. Such knowledge is usually not made explicit, but is often useful and powerful. Intuitive knowledge contrasts with the "formal knowledge" children are taught in school. Bamberger defines formal knowledge as a commonly accepted set of well-articulated descriptions of experience, which may have little connection with the knowledge individuals regularly apply in their everyday lives.

The teachers in Bamberger's study engaged in activities to help them distinguish between their intuitive ways of making sense of various phenomena and the formal knowledge they had been taught in school. One goal of the project was to develop practical strategies to help children connect their intuitive ways of understanding experience with the conventional formulas one needs to know to suceed in school and society.

In the traditional role of teachers as imparters of knowledge, the teachers in the project found it very difficult to not superimpose their own values of what "should be." "Formal knowledge," to the teachers meant not *one among many ways of knowing;* it was the "right" way. What Bamberger called "formal knowledge," the teachers called "right answers." These teachers were not different from other teachers or adults in general in trying to help youngsters be successful in society.

Yet in all our good intentions for children, we are often too quick to invalidate a child's way of knowing something. One youngster in

Lamperts' report asked, "Does Dataman have eyes?" This was not a silly question, as perceived by the teacher. Dataman, a hand-held computer game, looks like a robot and lets the children know if answers are right or not. The child may well have been equating the robot to a human being – for don't we talk about computers as having a memory, a brain, and in some cases, a voice? To help the child make the connection with what was intuitively meaningful, the teacher could explore the implications of the child's thoughts about the mechanical toy, perhaps by asking, "How do you think Dataman can tell what your answers are?" In this way, the children can be encouraged to expand their thinking. Then they and their way of thinking are not put down by a formal knowledge "right answer."

Bruner, in *The Process of Education*, expressed similar thoughts when he said, "Unfortunately, the formalism of school learning has somehow devalued intuition." When encouraged to use intuitive thinking or to make "educated guesses," the thinker's results might be right or wrong. (Results of intuitive thinking can be checked out by analytical thinking.) Bruner emphasizes that fostering self-confidence in children is necessary if they are to have the courage and willingness to make some honest mistakes in their efforts to solve problems. Children are unwilling to run the risk of perhaps being wrong if they are insecure or lack self-confidence. Certainly, we need to help children trust themselves and feel confident in exploring their inner knowledge.

In his book *Anatomy of Reality: Merging of Intuition and Reason*, Jonas Salk (1983) supports the idea of encouraging intuitive processes:

> *A new way of thinking is now needed to deal with our present reality, which is sensed more sensitively through intuition than by our capacity to observe and to reason objectively. Our subjective responses (intuitional) are more sensitive and more rapid than our mind works. We first sense and then we reason why. Intuition is an innate quality, but it can be developed and cultivated.*

Salk goes on to say that intuition may be seen as a continuation or extension of "natural" processes, like instinct, for example. Reason may be seen as that which man adds to explain his intuitive sense. Both intuition and reason play powerful roles in our lives. He states that intuition must be allowed free rein and be allowed to play. Then reason can select from the patterns that emerge.

Unless we allow that free play in children, they will become accustomed to not using or trusting their intuitions. In comparing a younger and an older child, Robert Kegan (1982) in *The Evolving Self* talks about the difference in these children's view of fantasy and reality. The younger child seems to make no differentiation between inner and outer thoughts: Younger children will engage parents in the middle of a conversation that they have already started on their own. It is as if they have trouble keeping track of which portions of a conversation they actually have had with you and/or which they have only imagined with you, or as if they take it for granted that their private thinking is as public and monitored as their spoken thinking. Older children never do this, and, indeed, in their cultivation of a sense of privacy and self-possession, they seem to have "sealed up" this psychic cavity.

Kegan states that at about the age of seven a child takes on the social role of a child, i.e., a child who will grow up to be an adult, a child in relation to parents. The child's structure seems to "come inside" to be covered over, rather than being constantly open and somehow shared with the world. Children's reality at this age is their perception of themselves as separate from objects and other people, where earlier their world was dominated by subjectivity and a sense of connection between their inner self, and thinking, and everything outside. What's more, the children begin to realize that others' perceptions might be different from their own. They make a shift to being a separate entity in the world, and that world is not subject to them. As Kegan puts it:

> *As a toddler . . . in filling my language with "me" and "mine," I am expressing my sense that* I *am; but as a seven-year-old, in conquering the role, I am developing a sense of what I am, a self with properties that persists through time.*

It seems, therefore, that at the age of approximately seven (from the developmentalist point of view), children break from an important alliance with their inner way of knowing and from the sharing of it openly with their surrounding world. Without this sharing and having it externally validated as meaningful and important, it's no wonder intuition atrophies. The William Wordworth poem "Intimations of Immortality" suggests this very same thing:

> *. . . Shades of the prison house (worldly existence) begin to close*
> *Upon the growing boy . . .*

Barbara Clark (1979), an educator known for her work with gifted children, suggests that adults can encourage children to use their intuitive abilities by themselves demonstrating that they value and trust their own intuitions. She suggests you listen to yourself and act upon that information. Also, you can observe and discover children's inner rhythms and ideas, and find ways to draw out their ideas and show that you respect and value them. The inhibition of intuitive ability begins by children finding intuition ridiculed or devalued by those people important to them.

Clark offers the following approaches for encouraging children to use their intuitive abilities. She suggests that, prior to employing any of them, some relaxation technique be used.

1. *Fantasy and Imagery*
   Reading or telling stories, making up plays, finishing open-ended stories, and playing "let's pretend" games all provide opportunities for development. Encourage children to share their fantasies through poems, plays, journals and books. Guided fantasies are also very effective.
2. *Feeling Energy*
   These activities help youngsters become aware of the human being as one of many forms of energy in the universe. The human system is surrounded by energy moving at varying rates of speed and with different intensity. You can help youngsters become aware of their own field of energy and its effect on others. Two activities Clark suggests are:

   Hand Ball. After a relaxation exercise, ask the youngsters to place their hands close together, then apart, until they can feel the energy between them. Some will feel it as heat, some as denser air. Maintaining this distance apart, move the hands in a parallel, circular motion with one hand preceding the other round and round, as your feet would move when pedaling a bicycle. Now stop and again feel the energy between your hands. Then pass the "ball" of energy to someone else. Encourage the children to talk about the experience.

(Each of us has space surrounding us that is filled with our own energy; and into which we feel uncomfortable allowing few people into our space. Exploring our own personal space provides more information about our energy field.)

   Space Walking. Ask youngsters to walk around the room in any direction and then stop and face someone else. Ask them to stand 2-4 feet away from their partner. Have the partners move slowly towards each other and stop when they feel themselves in their partner's space. Have them back up and move forward a few times. Then have them try it with their backs to each other. Let them try it with other people and see if how well they know each partner makes a difference.

Clark (1979) offers three basic steps in developing intuitive abilities: quiet the mind, focus attention, use a receptive attitude. She stresses that, although the preceding seems simplistic, the steps need to be valued and practiced for them to be effective. And again, the adult also must engage in and value them, setting a model for youngsters. She suggests the following procedure:

Have the youngsters sit quietly and comfortably, asking them to relax and allow their minds to be very quiet. Explain that this activity is difficult, so that they won't be disappointed with themselves if they are not totally successful the first time. When a thought comes to mind, ask them to allow it to be surrounded by a soft cloud and drift away. At first, try this for three to five minutes, gradually working up to ten minutes.

When ten minutes is possible, ask them to quiet their minds and "see" a large screen in front of their closed eyelids. Have them "put" a square on the screen, then a circle, then a triangle. In the triangle, place numbers, one at a time. Do this with several numbers.

Now, once again on a blank screen, allow a picture to emerge. After a while, ask the students to share the picture by talking with a partner, or have them draw or write about their experiences.

Pearce (1985) makes a strong point about capitalizing on "prime time" for children's development of intuition. He compares it to Dream Time, a mind-set by which Australian aborigines have operated for more than 30,000 years. By shifting back and forth from the present moment into Dream Time, the aborigine had at his disposal information "closed to our senses five" as the poet William Blake said. This is that capacity of intuition that appears around age four and disappears at about age seven for lack of such activities as Dream Time and aborigine-type models. By means of Dream Time, the aborigine knew the location and direction of travel of those animals he was allowed, by his particular clan, to kill, even though those animals might be miles away. He knew where to intercept the animals, and he knew the location of water in the desert, not by some acute ground reading of exterior clues, but by shifting into Dream Time.

Pearce (1985) relates that the aborigine believed that every man, woman, animal, blade of grass, water hole, or tree had a counterpart, a subtle or *dream* image. The plan of the world is laid out in this dream form and enacted now, in the physical world. A perfect coordination and cooperation with Dream Time assures man a perfect relation with the force that shapes our world, with creation itself. The aborigine was bonded with the earth. He maintained a state of unity between earth and self. He provided his children with models that stimulated and nurtured intuitive functions at appropriate times in their lives.

The aborigines paid attention to the two most important times in their children's lives for this development, from four to seven and from seven to eleven. A big ceremony, similar to some sort of rite of passage, was not made out of this attention. Rather, they were role models of Dream Time behavior and they encouraged children to practice it, too.

Pearce (1985) emphasizes that it is crucial to provide opportunities for the development of the right cerebral hemisphere, where intuitive capabilities are lodged. He says we have an explosive, universal longing for expression, and that this expression for children comes through play, storytelling, and let's pretend. We must relearn, states Pearce, that nature's didactic method is play, the re-creative play of childhood that alone leads to the divine creative play of maturity.

We owe our children the chance to be all that they might become. The late Donald MacKinnon (1978), a researcher who identified the personality characteristics of highly creative people, discussed the kinds of educational processes appropriate for strengthening youngsters' two perceptual modes: sense perception and intuitive perception. To strengthen and reinforce sense perception (often at the expense of intuitive development), teachers use learning, learning of facts for the sake of fact-learning alone, repeated drill of material, too much emphasis on facts related to other facts, and excessive concern with memorizing. To strengthen the disposition to intuitive perception as well as intuitive thinking, MacKinnon suggests teachers emphasize the transfer of training from one subject to another; the searching for common principles in terms of which facts from quite different domains of knowledge can be related; the stressing of analogies, similies and metaphors; exercises in imaginative play; and training in moving away from just facts in order to see larger contexts.

Both types of perception are important. The problem is that educational practices over-emphasize sense perception. In MacKinnon's words:

> ... what I am proposing is not that in teaching one disdain acute and accurate sense perceptions, but that one use it to build upon, leading the student always to an intuitive understanding of that which he experiences.

References

Bamberger, J., et al. (1981). *An experiment in teacher development: Final report.* Washington, DC: National Institute of Education, March.

Bastik, T. (1982). *Intuition: How we think and act.* NY: John Wiley & Sons.

Bruner, J. (1977). *The process of education.* Cambridge, MA: Harvard University Press.

Clark, B. (1979). *Growing up gifted.* Columbus, OH: Charles E. Merrill Publishing Company.

Kegan, R. (1982). *The evolving self.* Cambridge, MA: Harvard University Press.

Lampert, M. (1984). Teaching about thinking and thinking about teaching. *Journal of Curriculum Studies, 16* (1), 1-18.

MacKinnon, D. W. *In search of human effectiveness.* Buffalo, NY: Creative Education Foundation/Creative Synergenic Associates.

Pearce, J. C. (1985). *The magical child matures.* NY: E. P. Dutton.

Salk, J. (1983). *Anatomy of reality: Merging of intuition and reason.* NY: Columbia University Press.

Wordsworth, W. (1956). Intimations of immortality. In M. A. Neville & M. J. Herzberg (Eds.), *This England.* NY: Rand McNally & Company.

CHAPTER FIVE

Intuition in the Creative Arts

Intuition in art is not limited to the creative vision or images which are subsequently given form. The creative process itself is guided by the artist's intuition that lets him or her know when it is 'right'... Unlike the mathematician, the artist does not need to rationally justify his or her intuitive perceptions of what is 'right.'

Frances Vaughan
Awakening Intuition

Jerome Bruner (1961) reported that at the University of Buffalo there is a collection of successive drafts of poems written by leading contemporary poets. In examining them, one is struck by the immediate sense of the rightness of a revision a poet has made – but it is often difficult for the reader and the poet alike – or impossible – to say why the revision is better than the original.

In a study of writers and visual artists conducted by Jacob Getzels of the University of Chicago, it was found that the most successful artists seemed not to know what they were doing until a form emerged late in the process. Getzels said that the artists' actions reveal that they are working in a goal-directed way, but without full conscious awareness of what the goal is.

Perhaps this sense of "rightness," this moving toward a goal which is not clearly defined, is part of the feeling many artists attribute to being not creators, but rather transmitters. Max Ernst in "Inspiration to Order" (Ghiselin, 1952) discusses the process of *frottage* or "automatic writing," where the author is present as a spectator, indifferent or impassioned, at the birth of his/her own work and observes the phases of his/her own development. He said the process simply depends on "intensifying the mind's capacity for nervous excitement, using the appropriate technical means, excluding all conscious directing of the mind (toward reason, taste, or morals) and reducing to a minimum the part played by the 'author' of the work." Ernst went on to say that just as the poet's place (since the celebrated "Letter of a Clairvoyant") consists in writing at the dictation of something that makes itself articulate within, so the artist's role is to gather together and then give out that which makes itself *visible* within.

It has been said that artists create the structure of their psychic life by means of their works. Carl Jung (1949), the psychologist, stated that the work in process becomes the poet's fate and determines his psychic development. It is not Goethe who creates *Faust*, but *Faust* which creates Goethe. That may be a clue as to why artists seem vague at the beginning of a creative process, and why it's the intuitive sense of rightness that keeps them going.

Others have attested to their creative processes and subsequent products coming from somewhere or something else. This is an account of Mozart describing himself as hearing melodies in his head:

> When I feel well and in a good humor, or when I am taking a drive or walking after a good meal, or in the night when I cannot sleep, thoughts crowd into my mind as easily as you could wish. Whence and how do they come? I do not know and I have nothing to do with it. Those which please me, I keep in my head and hum them; at least others have told me that I do so. Once I have my theme, another melody comes, linking itself to the first one, in accordance with the needs of the composition as a whole: the counterpoint, the part of each instrument, and all these melodic fragments at last produce the entire work: Then my soul is on fire with inspiration, if however nothing occurs to distract my attention (Ghiselin, 1952).

There have been numerous testimonies given by creative artists about intuitive modes that helped them open up, set the stage, and ready themselves for the creative process to begin. They apparently recognized intuition as the first stage of the creative process; they welcomed modes that were dominated by intuition rather than reason. This is achieved by invoking a passive/receptive state entered into willingly and with anticipation. This is a pleasure state where the artist feels some resolve will occur. The pre-intuitive mode is often characterized by an agony of indecision and avoidance. It is the same as not having a specific goal, but knowing that something needs to be done. To get himself into an intuitive mode, Cellist, Pablo Casals, started each day by playing several Bach fugues on the piano.

John Curtis Gowan, a psychologist, conducted some major research on 19th century composers, attempting to discern any commonalities in their processes of inspiration. He reports on their experiences of "inner listening," turning inward to their own inner resources. He said of these particular composers that, since most of them were orthodox Christians, their words were clothed in religious forms. Brahms said (Abell, 1964):

> When I feel the urge (to compose) I begin by appealing directly to my Maker . . . I feel vibrations . . . which assume the form of distinct mental images. Straightaway the ideas flow in upon me, directly from God . . . I have to be in a semi-trance condition to get such results – a condition when the conscious mind is in temporary abeyance, and the subconscious is in control, for it is through the subconscious mind . . . that the inspiration comes.

Puccini stated (Abell, 1964):

> I make a fervent demand for and from the Power that created me. This demand or prayer must be coupled with full expectation that this higher aid will be granted me . . . The music of this opera (Madame Butterfly) was dictated to me by God: I was merely instrumental in putting it on paper and communicating it to the public . . .

Playwright Jean Cocteau declared that he did not feel that inspiration falls from heaven. On the contrary, he felt it to be the result of a profound indolence and incapacity to put to work certain forces in ourselves.

> These unknown forces work deep within us . . . They burden us and oblige us to conquer the kind of somnolence in which we indulge ourselves like invalids who try to prolong dreams and dread resuming contact with reality . . . in short when the work that makes itself in us and in spite of us demands to be born . . . at this moment consciousness must take precedence over the unconscious . . . and it becomes necessary to find the means which permit the informed work to take form, to render it visible at all (Cocteau in Ghiselin, 1952).

When English poet Edith Sitwell (1958) was responding to criticism of the obscurity of some poetry, she said, "*Sometimes the difficulty may be the result of the poet's inspirations not having completely found its way out of the unconscious in which all poetry is conceived.*" She, however, defends that apparent obscurity in a piece called "The Poet's Vision" by saying that it is part of the poet's work to give each man his own view of the world — show him what he sees but does not know that he sees:

> *The great artist in each of the arts retains* spiritually *the child's wondering vision of the glories of the world. His vision, his hearing, are closer to the quintessence of reality than any other vision or hearing.*

Sitwell's comments are similar to what painter Max Bechman said. *"My aim is always to get hold of the magic of reality . . . to make the invisible visible through reality . . . "* (Beckman, 1941). Famous painter Paul Klee states, an artist " *. . . does nothing other than gather and pass on what comes to him from the depths. He neither serves nor rules . . . he transmits"* (Klee, 1948).

Intuitive powers allow an artist, or anyone for that matter, to tap into the inner realms of consciousness. Carl Jung (1964) maintains that, when we speak of the unconscious, there are two layers of the unconscious: the personal and the collective. The personal contains all the psychic material of memories, repressed experiences, and certain impressions. The collective unconscious, on the other hand, refers to contents that are common to everyone, the ancient and universal thought forms of humanity. On a much deeper level, this layer of the unconscious contains the inherited possibility of physical functioning. These are universal, primordial images which Jung called "archetypes," symbols that appear universally in cultural myths and legends. It is through archetypes that your experiences can be interpreted and there can be greater understanding of what is happening in the world. Jung claims that it is through intuition that you can tune into this collective unconscious. A part of the power of the collective unconscious is its ability to help us understand our universe to get closer to the inner wisdom of humankind.

In *The Magic of Tone and the Art of Music,* Dane Rudhyar (1982) says, . . . real wisdom can only be reached through intuition. Intuition is a mode of supersensible perception, a spiritual "seeing." The intellectual mind cogitates, discusses, and argues about what might be, and can only come to a conclusion it already knows. But intuition directly perceives what *is*. Far more than knowledge, it is understanding.

The artist is concerned with discovering truth and gaining wisdom about humanity and the universe. Intuition allows one to draw from that vast storehouse of unconscious knowledge, the personal and the collective.

Art is very apparent in the practice of Zen. Zen philosophy asserts that enlightenment (the realization of truth and wisdom) manifests itself in everyday affairs and has enormous influence on all aspects of the traditional way of life. Art is very much a part of Eastern life, much more so than in the West, since art has a direct connection with seeking enlightenment. Besides the arts of painting, caligraphy, garden design and various crafts, other arts are important, such as the ceremonial activities of serving tea or arranging flowers and the martial arts of archery, swordsmanship and judo. Capra (1975) says, "*each of these activities is known in Japan as a 'do,' that is, a tao or 'way' toward enlightenment. They all explore various characteristics of the Zen experience and can be used to train the mind and bring it into contact with the ultimate reality.*" In each of the art forms ritualistic, deliberate movements are required. All of these arts are expressions of the spontaneity, simplicity and total presence of mind that are characteristic of the Zen way of life. Capra goes on, "*While they all require a perfection of techniques, real mastery is only achieved when technique is transcended and the art becomes an 'artless art' growing out of the unconscious.*" All of the forms are designed to develop the intuitive mind so that the individual might reach into the depths of his or her unconscious in seeking enlightenment.

The experience of aesthetic insight – that is, of creating an aesthetic unity – is a strong emotional experience, in some ways comparable to what psychologist Abraham Maslow has called "peak experiences." The artist feels as though he or she has touched the universal, and that the newly created unity seems to have incorporated the universal and become a "concrete universal" that transcends space and time. As Silvano Arieti (1976) states in *Creativity: The Magic Synthesis,*

> . . . *the quality of universality seems to come from two achievements: the enlargement of reality that everybody will acknowledge and the transformation of an endocept into a conscious and vivid experience in the inner reality of man.*

It's not only the artist who benefits from the aesthetic insight which produces the creative product. In art, the *spectator* hopes to, and very often does, experience – at least vicariously – what the artist has experienced and expressed. It seems possible, then, that the peak experiences of which Maslow speaks are a probability for both the artist and the spectator. True works of art nourish the spirit, and the spectator hears an answering chord within. Such emotional chords deepen the feeling of the spectator, and help him or her come closer to that sense of value in the inner self and its connections to the universe.

References

Abell, A. M. (1964). *Talks with the great composers.* Garmisch-Partenkirchen, Germany: G. E. Schroeder-Verlatz. (In Gowan, 1977).
Arieta, S. (1976). *Creativity: The magic synthesis.* NY: Basic Books.
Beckman, M. (1941). *On my painting.* NY: Valentine.
Bruner, J. (1961). *The process of education.* Cambridge, MA: Harvard University Press.
Capra, F. (1975). *The tao of physics.* Berkeley, CA: Shambhala.
Cocteau, J. (1952). The process of inspiration. In B. Ghiselin (Ed.), *The creative process.* NY: Mentor Books.
Ernst, M. (1982). Inspiration to order. In B. Ghiselin (Ed.), *The creative process.* NY: Mentor Books.
Gowan, J. C. (1977). Creative inspiration in composers. *Journal of Creative Behavior, 11* (4), 249-255.
Hampden-Turner, C. (1981). The dynamic unities of Carl G. Jung. In *Maps of the mind.* NY: Collier Books.
Holmes, E. (1952). Life of Mozart. In B. Ghiselin (Ed.), *The creative process.* NY: Mentor Books.
Jung, C. G. (1949). Psychology and literature. In *Modern man in search of a soul.* NY: Harcourt, Brace & Company.
Jung, C. G. (1964). *Man and his symbols.* Garden City, NY: Doubleday.
Kandensky, W. (1967). Concerning the spiritual in art. In J. Hall & B. Ulanor (Eds.), *Modern culture and the arts.* NY: McGraw-Hill.
Klee, P. (1948). *On art.* London, England: Faber & Faber.
Noddings, N. & Shore, P. J. (1984). *Awakening the inner eye.* NY: Teachers College Press.
Rudhar, D. (1982). *The magic of tone and the art of music.* Boulder, CO: Shambhala Publications, Inc.
Sitwell, E. (1958). The poet's vision. In R. Thruelsen & J. Kobler (Eds.), *Adventures of the mind.* NY: Vintage Books.
Vaughan, F. E. (1979). *Awakening intuition.* NY: Anchor Press.

CHAPTER SIX

Intuition and Psychology

A human being is not one thing among others; things determine each other, but man is ultimately self-determining. What he becomes within limits of endowment and environment — he has made out of himself.

Viktor E. Frankl, M.D.
Man's Search For Meaning

Psychology is concerned with the thoughts and ideas people hold about their life, as well as feelings and moods. In psychology, the inner world is extremely important. With the current increased interest in studying human consciousness (Gardner, 1983; Sternberg, 1982; Rogers, 1961), dialogue over the long standing conflict on the role of the unconscious has once again surfaced. Sigmund Freud (1943) theorized that the unconscious was negative and its role inhibited the full development of the individual. To Freud, the unconscious was replete with unpleasant memories and repressed thoughts which were locked away from conscious awareness by a type of internal gatekeeper or censor.

On the other hand, according to Myers (1903), who was a contemporary of Freud, the unconscious is the *source* of intuition and creativity. For the unconscious, Myers used the metaphor of a gold mine. He saw the unconscious as the source of cultured treasures, art, religious ideas and inventions that are needed and valued by civilization. In his book entitled *Human Personality and Its Survival of Bodily Death*, he suggested a number of areas that required study, such as unconscious processes, sleep and dreams, hypnosis, creativity and inspiration, and survival of the personality after physical death.

Today, we see many of these topics gaining in scientific respectability. In fact, there is a growing sentiment that the unconscious is well able to harbor both negative and positive points of view. Some memories and data are unpleasant and threatening, and lie hidden away from the conscious mind; yet another type of deep intuition knows the way to create wholesome development and growth, and leads the person in a positive direction. When a person and these two poles of one's being are integrated, deep personal breakthroughs can be accomplished.

As people experience personal breakthroughs, they often describe inner listening or inner discoveries. Some report communication from an audible voice or the capacity to hear the speech of the other self. Many artists and inventors have used the metaphor of tapping into a flowing source "an underground river" of creative imagination, or opening the mind's gate. Scientists and methematicians have also spoken of a lightning flash of intuition. Others described a channel that may come from a creative unconscious within the psyche or from some external source.

A number of techniques or therapies have been developed to increase understanding of a person's state of mind and to encourage personal integration. Many of these contemporary therapies use visualization techniques to tap the intuitive mind. Specific activities are offered here for the reader to experience.

At the turn of the century, Freud suggested that, if we got in touch with our images, it would cause a release that could bring greater personal awareness and help stimulate basic growth processes in the inner world. Both Freud (1943) and Jung (1964) found that bringing certain emotionally-charged images to awareness often relieved neurotic symptoms and made the person's inner world whole. By experiencing the basic images, the person felt better and was able to grow emotionally.

The first doctor to elicit such images from a patient was Dr. Joseph Breuer, credited by Freud with the creation of psychoanalysis. Dr. Breuer found that when his patient was made to remember situations and the associative connections under which they first appeared, catharsis took place, and the patient's symptoms disappeared.

Freud (1960) attested to the value of visualization by stating that thinking in pictures more closely approximated the unconscious processes, than did thinking in words.

Carl Jung placed great importance on images in his theories. Jung tried to locate the images which were concealed in the emotions. In his book *Memories, Dreams and Reflections*, Jung (1963) reported that the type of inner study required to study images could be fear producing. One account of his searching is particularly revealing. In 1913 he reported a visualization: while seated at his desk, he felt the ground give way beneath his feet. He plunged into great dark depths and felt a sense of panic. Then suddenly, his feet landed on a soft, sticky mass and he perceived himself in complete darkness. When his eyes grew accustomed to the dark, he noted a leathery, skinned dwarf standing in front of a deep cave.

Jung's visualization is similar to a common guided fantasy or image journey (as suggested in Chapter Three) in which the reader is asked to confront a wise old man to tap into the intuitive mind.

Jung reported that the years in which he pursued his inner images were the most important in his life. His goal was to reach a point where he could visualize freely and easily.

Active Imagination

Jung developed a technique, which he called active imagination, to enable his patients to benefit from their inner images. In active imagination, the person is asked to meditate and to try and remain free from any goal or program. Then the person is asked to invite images to flow and to watch them without interfering. Jung also suggests that it is helpful to interact with the images, and then subsequently discuss the experience with the therapist. Jung's psychological technique is different from Freud's in that it is more likely to bring forth imagination, rather than memory images.

Jung used the term archetypal to label images that were experienced during active imagination. He described these images as primordial and part of man's mind. Examples of archetypes include the hero journey, the initiation ritual, the earth mother, and beauty and the beast. Jung stated that these archetypal images were first experienced by ancient man; modern man could experience the same archetypes through visualization. Through reflection, we can better understand them.

Induced Dreams

Sacerdote (1968), a psychotherapist from the United States, developed a technique called induced dreams. He would hypnotize his patients and suggest that they begin an interesting, possibly strange dream with a pleasant conclusion that would help them solve their past and present problems. Following the dream, Sacerdote would use free association techniques to help the patients interpret their dreams. He would then again hypnotize the patients and suggest that they have a dream related to the first one. By this technique, Sacerdote could gather data on a succession of dreams dealing with related themes.

A technique congruent with that of Sacerdote is one developed by Beck (1970), called forward time projection.

Forward Time Projection

In forward time projection, the patient is requested to see himself in a present situation and to visualize being in the same situation three months, six months, a year, or even five years hence. This technique enables the patient to see beyond the moment of anxiety and fear to a time when the source of anxiety is in the past and the problem has been resolved. Forward time projections relieve tension and encourage the patients to place their anxiety into perspective.

Systematic Desensitization

Joseph Wolpe (1969), a prominent behavioral therapist developed the technique of systematic desensitization. He suggested that the patient relax and visualize a series of situations related to the source of anxiety or phobia. The patient then was asked to create a hierarchy and rank order the visualizations from the most distressing to those least distressing. Wolpe reports on a patient who had a phobia for cats. She ranked her visualizations in this order: a visualization of a sunny day and talking with a friend who mentions the word cat (mildly distressing); coming across a picture of a cat in a magazine; a good friend sitting with a cat two blocks away; a cat in the next room; a cat in an airline's travel cage in the same room; a cat sleeping in a chair across the room; and, finally, a cat sitting on the patient's lap (most distressing).

Wolpe instructs his patients to visualize that scene in the hierarchy which is least anxiety producing. He then asks them to relax and see the visualization in which there is little anxiety. They are instructed to visualize the next scene without anxiety. Through such exercises, the patient is trained to replace feelings of anxiety with the pleasant sense of relaxation.

Wolpe used the progressive relaxation techniques of Jacobson (1965), an American physician specializing in muscle physiology with emphasis on relaxation. An exercise similar to those of Jacobson for becoming aware of tension and relaxation is: Rest your arm on a flat surface and raise your hand by bending it up at the wrist. When your hand is raised, the muscles on top of your forearm below the elbow will be contracted, tense. Let your hand go limp. Those muscles are now relaxed and your hand will drop. The feeling of tension or contraction when you raise your hand is subtle. If you bend your hand back too far, you may feel strain in the opposing muscles of your arm. If you don't feel the upper forearm tension at first, alternately raise your hand in a slow, even motion and then let it go limp. Rest the fingers of your other hand lightly on top of your forearm in order to feel the muscle contract under your fingers.

By using exercises such as these, you can become aware of tension and relaxation in any muscle in your body. Jacobson felt that the mind also can naturally become relaxed and clear as the body becomes more relaxed (Jacobson, 1965).

Cognitive Therapy

An example of cognitive therapy is provided by Goldfried (1971) in his work on the use of coping skills. Here the patient is asked to imagine a stressful situation and to imagine coping with anxiety. At each stage, anxiety is tolerated through the use of relaxation techniques that cope with the arousal of anxiety caused by the images. Mahoney and Arnoff (1974) report on covert modeling therapy in which the patient serves as his/her own model and, in a series of imagined sequences, tries out and evaluates coping strategies.

Implosive Therapy

Stampfl (1967) developed the implosive technique in the 1960s. He stated that, by making a person visualize the most anxiety producing situation they could, the person would find the imagined experience less anxiety producing than the person feared. In this manner, they would learn that they can control their thoughts.

LeCron (1961) reports on a number of therapies that can be called age regression. You might want to try those included here.

Age Regression

In age regression therapy the patient is asked to re-experience, using all five senses, a situation that has previously happened (LeCron, 1961). This is a modified activity: See yourself floating on a magic carpet. As you look below, you see a broad river which is the river of time. The past is upstream. The carpet is directed to move upstream. There is a milepost below with a number – the present date. The carpet moves further back and a second milestone is seen – the previous year. Speeding up, one milepost after another is passed. Have the carpet stop at the desired time and experience it with all five senses. What do you see, hear, feel, taste, and smell?

Another activity to try is: Visualize a large book open at the middle pages. This is the book of life. See the pictures on the pages and see the pages turning back rapidly, page by page, until you reach the one representing the desired date. Again experience this visualization with all five of your senses. What are you seeing, hearing, feeling, tasting, smelling?

Here is another activity: See a grandfather clock. The hands are moving counterclockwise. Below the face of the clock is a dial showing the month, date and year. As the hands turn backward, faster and faster, the dates on the dial change. Again, continue until you reach the desired time. Now what are you seeing, hearing, feeling, tasting, and smelling?

The therapies presented in this chapter are techniques based primarily on receptive visualization. They are successful because most people are open to their own memory and imagination. As images from the unconscious are brought to awareness, they can improve a person's state of mind and result in personal growth. Yet another group of therapies use more programming. In these techniques, the therapist provides specific suggestions for visual content and directions on how to manipulate and control the images.

Symbolic Consciousness

Happich, a German internist, developed a technique in the 1920s and 1930s called symbolic consciousness. He states that this level of consciousness lies between the conscious and the unconscious. At this level, we can experience the collective unconscious as expressed in symbols. Happich asks his patients to relax deeply and to imagine leaving the room and crossing fields to reach a meadow. He then asks his patients to describe in detail what they experience in the meadow.

Happich, as reported in Tart (1969), calls this activity the *meadow meditation.* He might suggest that the patients visualize climbing a mountain, and he asks them to describe the view. Or, he uses the *chapel meditation,* in which they enter a chapel, remain there and describe this meditation. Finally, there is the meditation where they visualize sitting on a bench by an old fountain, listening to the water.

Happich believed that, at the meditative level, the meadow, mountain, and chapel images go beyond everyday life and become archetypes or primordial symbols. He conceived of the meadow as a youthful Mother Nature, or the positive, creative side of a person's life; the ascent of a mountain represented our achieving psychic freedom. The forest represented the dark and fearful side of a person's nature and the chapel is the room in which the person is able to confront the central problems of life.

As part of this treatment, Happich also encouraged his patients to design a mandala with which they could psychically identify, and to try to integrate the meaning of the symbol into their psychic life.

Guided Affective Imagery

Guided affective imagery (GAI) was developed in the 1950s and 1960s. GAI calls for the patient to relax and imagine a meadow. Leuner (1969), who developed the technique at the University of Goettingern, encouraged the patient to develop a personal visual fantasy around the word "meadow." He used ten standard imaginary situations. The meadow represented a fresh start, the patient's present mood, the Garden of Eden or a patient's mother-child relationship.

After viewing the meadow, the patient was asked to find a path and follow it through a forest to a mountain. According to Leuner, the symbol of the mountain pertained to the patient's career and achievements. The patient was directed to look around the meadow, find a brook and follow it downstream to the ocean, or upstream to its source. The brook symbolized the flow of psychic energy and potential for emotional development. The brook or spring could also represent a magical healing fluid.

The patient was then asked to visualize a house and to explore the rooms in the house. The house is a symbol of the patient's personality onto which fears and wishes can be projected. Then the patient was instructed to return to the meadow and to visualize a close relative. The patient's description of the relative represented their emotional relationships. Next, the patient was to visualize sexual situations, followed by visualizations of a lion in a cage, jungle or desert. The lion represented aggressive tendencies. In the eighth situation, the patient was directed to visualize a person of their own sex. Leuner reported that patients usually visualize someone they would like to be. This visualization can help in working out personal identity.

In the ninth situation, the patient is to visualize being at a safe distance from the forest, and to watch for a creature to emerge. This visualization stimulates the emergence of symbolic figures such as witches, giants and monsters. In the tenth and final situation, the patient is requested to visualize a swamp in the corner of a meadow and to describe a figure emerging from it. This figure is symbolic of deeply repressed archaic sexual material.

If the patient shows fear, Happich suggests the therapist ask them to confront the creature, to feed it or attempt to make friends with it.

Leuner (1969) reports that his patients often gain control of the therapeutic process. He credits this to a spontaneous inner pacemaker, the influence of which on the treatment process can be invoked by the GAI method. He accomplishes this by asking the patient to allow himself to be guided by one of his own benign symbolic figures.

Leuner states that by helping people stimulate their imagination with these ten situations, he can diagnose a patient's illness and use this diagnosis as a basis for free association.

Symbolic Visualization

Roberto Assagioli, an Italian psychiatrist, developed the technique of symbolic visualization. His patients are asked to sit in a comfortable chair, close their eyes and relax. They are directed to visualize a number of symbols in their mind's eye.

Girard, a Los Angeles psychologist who uses symbolic visualization, reports that he used a group of symbols representing synthesis, integration and balance, such as sunflowers, a white dot at the center of a white circle, a cross, a five or six pointed white star, and various mandalas. The next group of symbols relates to harmonious group relations, such as two clasped hands. A third group represents masculinity and femininity, such as a shining sword or a golden cup. The fourth group, in which Gerard uses colors, symbolizes affective states. The patients are asked to picture themselves as a globe of light or a particular color. In addition, Gerard asks the patients to change images, like a seed becoming a tree or a worm becoming a butterfly.

These techniques are designed to help the patient find a visual image that corresponds to verbal thought. In this manner, images can be held in the mind as personal goals.

The late Assagioli called his symbolic visualization psychosynthesis, a holistic approach. He urged the use of guided imagery and kinesthetic imagery to evoke inner wisdom. Sometimes the process involved dialogue (visually imagined or acted out) with a figure that was designated as a source of wisdom, or an element of nature, or a sacred animal. The wisdom figure was usually invited to comment on various aspects of the client's life or to respond to certain provocative questions. Assagioli (1973) reported that patients were reassured to discover that they had within themselves a source of wisdom that they could use. Psychosynthesis asserts that, in learning to cooperate consciously with this deeper source of one's being, the individual can then experience the total fulfillment of human life. Assagioli (1973) in his book *The Act of Will* characterized his theory as an integration view of the human being.

Autogenic Training

Lindemann (1973) reports that, through passive concentration on autogenic formulas, the individual can self-induce an altered state of consciousness that teaches manipulation of the bodily functions through the mind. According to Lindemann, this results in the normalization of both physical and mental states.

In autogenic training, there is active participation, as the individual is encouraged to induce a sense of quieting through the use of affirmations. Examples of such so called peace formulas are:

1. I am calm and quiet.
2. Nothing around me is important.
3. My thoughts pass like clouds in the summer sky.

These peace formula affirmations can be followed by other more directional ones such as:

1. I have the wisdom to know what is right for me.
2. With every day that passes, I am getting a greater feeling of well-being, safety and security.
3. I am learning to picture myself the way I want to be.

Lindemann (1973) reports that patients who use autogenic training have a generalized sense of peace and an increased vividness of their dreams. In addition, their problems are solved with less anxiety. One patient reported that envisioning a white light around her body whenever needed made her feel less physically vulnerable.

Integration therapy incorporates many of the techniques of autogenic training.

Integration Therapy

Integration therapy was developed by Walter Urban in the 1970s. Urban (1978) describes integration therapy as involving the use of a combination of techniques derived from different therapeutic modalities, all working toward freeing one's natural energy and creativity.

Integration therapy incorporates some of Fritz Perls' ideas from Gestalt therapy, notably his emphasis on awareness and its vital importance. According to Perls, as each moment changes, awareness is always changing. Therefore, by becoming more aware the individual can be free to create.

An example of Gestalt therapy is to imagine the different roles of an incident. For example, an abusive childhood experience might be dealt with by having the individual image being the child, then becoming the abuser. More specifically, one can image a man hitting a dog, then become the man, the dog and then the stick. Each time, the individual is to describe the incident from the different points of view.

Psycho-Imagination Theory

Psycho-Imagination theory is a phenomenological and dialogical process with major emphasis on encouraging subjective meaning through the modality of awakening imagery and imagination. Psycho-imagination theory recognizes that people need to become aware of how they define themselves in relation to others and how they in turn define others.

This so called phenomenological "in-seeing" or "in-viewing" is a synthesis of the theories of R. D. Laing and Harry Stack Sullivan. Shorr (1981) in his chapter in *Handbook on Innovative Psychotherapies* describes in-viewing as: *How I see myself . . . . How I see you . . . . How I see you seeing me . . . . How you see me seeing you . . .*

Self-Image Theory

Shorr (1979), writing on the use of imagery as a method of self-observation, suggests the use of both spontaneous imagery and directed imagery. In 1976 Shorr founded a clinic in Los Angeles where he has developed projective tests using imagery and specific self-imagery techniques. Some examples of directed imagery are: Imagine there are two of you. Imagine kissing yourself or looking at yourself through a keyhole.

Through the use of creating dual images such as imagining two selves, two animals, two dolls, two forces or two impulses, the patient frequently identifies two parts of the self which are in conflict, and gains insight from these images. Insight is also gained in specific conflicts that may arise in self versus self or self versus another.

In addition, special imaging can help reveal layers of information. An activity you might want to try is the following: Imagine three doors, one on your left, one in front of you and one on your right. Open each door. What do you see, what do you do and what do you feel?

Lastly, there are a number of guided questions concerning self that can be used in self image theory (Shorr, 1981):

To whom are you accounting?
Never refer to me as _____.
Did (do) you make a difference to anyone?
Did (does) anyone acknowledge your existence?
How do (did) you make people aware of you?
Were (are) you ever believed?
What qualities did your parents deny in you?
How would you drive somebody out of their mind?

Eidetic Imagery Therapy

Early work in the area of eidetic imagery therapy was accomplished at the Marburg Institute of Psychotherapy under E. R. Jaensch in the 1900s. The eidetic was defined as a vivid visual image of a presented figure, which usually lingers for a duration, is localized in space, and positive in color.

A leader in the area of eidetic psychotherapy is Akhter Ahsen (1977), who was first to apply the concepts of interval eidetics to psychotherapy. He formulated his ideas in Pakistan in the 1950s. He states that eidetic images are developmental and pertain to key memories and fantasies associated with basic growth and conflict.

The developmental image has a somatic pattern and a meaning, as well as a visual component. In his three major books *Basic Concepts in Eidetic Psychotherapy* (1968), *Eidetic Parents Test and Analysis* (1972) and *Psycheye: Self Analytic Consciousness* (1977), Ahsen suggests that when a life activity has been traumatically nullified, its original is still available, whole and complete in the form of a picture. One of his major contributions to understanding Eidetic Imagery Psychotherapy is his work with the Visual Imagery Association, their national and international conferences and the *Journal of Visual Imagery,* which he edits.

This discussion of the varied therapies does not represent a state of confusion, but a struggle toward a new view of man's problems and inner way of knowing. Through repeated questioning and investigation, understanding can take place. The essence of this notion is captured in Zen Buddhism.

When there is enough faith, there is enough doubt, which is a great spirit of inquiry and when there is a spirit of inquiry, there is an illumination.

Zen Buddhism

References

Ahsen, A. (1968). *Basic concepts in eidetic psychotherapy.* NY: Brandon House.
Ahsen, A. (1972). *Eidetic parents test and analysis.* NY: Brandon House.
Ahsen, A. (1977). *Psyche-eye.* NY: Brandon House.
Assagioli, R. (1973). *The act of will.* NY: Viking Press.
Beck, A. T. (1970). Role of fantasies in psychotherapy and psychopathology. *Journal of Nervous Mental Disease, 150* (1), 3-17.
Frankl, V. E. (1984). *Man's search for meaning.* NY: Simon & Schuster.
Gardner, H. (1983). *Frames of mind.* NY: Basic Books.
Goldfried, M. (1971). Systematic desensitization as training in self-control. *Journal of Consulting and Clinical Psychology, 37* (28), 234.
Jacobson, E. (1965). *How to relax and have your baby.* NY: McGraw Hill.
LeCron, L. (1961). *Techniques of hypnotherapy.* NY: Julien Press.
Leuner, H. (1969). Guided affective imagery. *American Journal of Psychotherapy, 23* (1), 6.
Lindemann, H. (1973). *Relieve tensions the autogenic way.* NY: Wyden.
Mahoney, M. J. (1974). *Cognition and behavior modification.* Cambridge, MA: Ballinger.
Myers, F. W. (1903). *Human personality and its survival of bodily death.* NY: Longman's, Green.
Rogers, C. (1961). *On becoming a person.* Boston, MA: Houghton-Mifflin.
Sacerdote, P. (1968). Induced dreams. *American Journal of Clinical Hypnosis, 10* (3), 167-173.
Shorr, J. E. (1979). Imagery as a method of self-observation in therapy. *Imagery Bulletin of the American Association for Study of Mental Imagery, 2.*
Shorr, J. E. (1981). Psycho-imagination therapy. In R. Corsini (Ed.), *Handbook of innovative psychotherapies.* NY: Wiley & Sons.
Stampfl, T. & Lewis, D. J. (1967). Essentials of implosive therapy. *Journal of Abnormal Psychology, 72* (6), 496-503.
Sternberg, R. (1982). A revolutionary look at intelligence. *Gifted Children's Newsletter, 3* (11).
Tart, C. (1969). (Ed.). *Altered states of consciousness.* Garden City, NY: Doubleday.
Urban, W. (1978). *Integrative therapy. Foundations for holistic and self-healing.* Los Angeles, CA: The Guild of Tutors Press.
Wolpe, J. (1969). *The practice of behavior therapy.* NY: Pergammon Press.

CHAPTER SEVEN

Intuition in the Sciences and Mathematics

The really valuable thing is intuition.

Albert Einstein
The Evolution of Physics

Contemporary cognitive psychologists are exploring imagery as an integral part of the way the brain functions, with particular emphasis on creative solutions generated in an out-of-conscious awareness process. These solutions often appear in awareness through imagery. Scientists who are trained observers are often quick to note this type of quasi-conscious learning and as their visions continue toward a coherent structural concept, illumination takes place (Kedrov, 1957; Muir, 1966; Vernon, 1970).

This chapter explores the use of imagery in tapping into the intuitive, with specific examples of scientists such as Mendeleev, Howe, Bohr, Kepler, Loewi, Kekule, Tesla and a number of selected mathematicians namely Poincaire, Ramanujan, Gauss and Pascal who experienced an inner way of knowing. In addition, we will explore several of the scientific community's new thinkers such as Pribram, Bohm, Capra and Salk and the importance of the science of human consciousness as championed by Edgar Mitchell.

Researching this chapter was an exciting process, for it led us to autobiographies, memorandum, diaries and classic studies on genius which captured moments of inspiration and illumination. As we talk with our colleagues, we note a growing interest in intuition in a number of diverse fields such as psychology, sociology, anthropology, biology, medicine, physics and computer science.

Sorokin, in his *Psychic Sourcebook,* summarizes this new development and interest by saying that, side-by-side with the subconscious (or unconscious) and conscious levels in human personality, a third stratum, the supraconscious, is gaining increasing recognition. He states that the supraconscious energies are the beginning of discoveries and inventions and include precognition and cognitive and creative intuition.

Moments of Inspiration

In examining moments of inspiration, remember that considerable preparation preceded the act. Kedrov (1957) reports that in 1869 Mendeleev went to bed after a particularly exhausting day, still struggling to conceptualize a method of categorizing the elements based on their atomic weights. Mendeleev dreamed he saw a table with all the elements in place on it. Upon awakening, he wrote them down, with only one correction being necessary. Needless to say, Mendeleev went to bed with a prepared mind.

Another example is that of Howe, as reported in the 1924 edition of *A Popular History of American Invention* by Kaempffert. Howe was working on his invention of the sewing machine and was making the needles with a hole in the middle of the shank. He had been working around the clock on his invention. One night he dreamed that he was captured by a tribe of savages. The warriors made a hollow square formation around him and led him to a place of execution. Suddenly, he noted that, near the heads of the spears each guard carried, were eye-shaped holes. Aha! What he needed was a needle with an eye near the point. When he awoke from his dream, he constructed a model of the eye pointed needle and he created a successful product – the lockstitch sewing machine.

Still another example is that of Niels Bohr and Sir Frederick Grant Banting as reported by Talamonti (1975) in *Forbidden Universe*. Bohr, a physicist, dreamed of a planetary system as a model for atoms as well as celestial bodies. Upon awakening, he formulated the Bohr model of atomic structure and consequently won a Nobel Prize. Sir Frederick Grant Banting dreamed about the mass production of insulin and joined a long list of so-called life-saving inventors.

Otto Loewi (1960), a physiologist, won a Nobel Prize in physiology and medicine. He discovered and demonstrated that the characteristic activity of nerve impulses is both a chemical and an electrical event. He came up with the idea during a conversation with a colleague. Yet, it was seventeen years later before the idea re-surfaced, this time in a dream. He reports that the night before Easter Sunday in 1920 he awoke and wrote a few notes. Then he fell asleep again. In the morning, the notes could not be deciphered. The next night at three o'clock the idea returned. It was the design of an experiment to test the hypothesis of chemical transmission. Loewi got up immediately and went to his lab, where he conducted a simple experiment on a frog's heart using his dream design. The results became the foundation of the nervous impulse theory of chemical transmission.

One of the most famous dream-inspired scientific breakthroughs is that of August Kekule von Stradonitz, known as Kekule (Harman & Rheingold, 1984). Kekule, a Flemish professor, lived in London and had been thinking and experimenting for years about possible ways that molecules connect to one another. The first of two key visions came to Kekule while he was riding on a streetcar. He saw two smaller atoms united to form a pair and a larger one embracing two smaller ones. Still larger atoms kept hold of three or four smaller atoms, all the while whirling in a giddy dance. The larger ones formed a chain. Kekule spent part of the night copying his dream forms on paper.

His second dream occurred several years later while he dozed in a chair. Again the atoms whirled before him. This time, the smaller groups were in the background. His mental eye distinguished larger structures of manifold conformation: long rows sometimes more closely fitted together, all twining and twisting in snakelike motion. One of the snakes seized the tail of another and the form whirled in front of his eyes.

Benzene is a cycle (or ring) structure; the carbon chain at the molecular core of the compound forms a chain that swallows its own tail. Kekule and the other scientists' unconscious processors had access to the data which allowed them to make significant contributions to the field of science by translating the symbol into workable scientific language.

Another example is the inventor Nikola Tesla. Tesla (1919) invented the electric power grid into which the wall socket taps. Tesla's invention of the alternating current dynamo and power transmission system made the electric age possible. Tesla kept detailed notes of his flashes of insight and he deliberately learned to cultivate visualization.

Tesla reports that at seventeen he found that he was easily able to visualize inventions. He would construct, modify and even operate his hypothetical devices by visualizing them. Once, he was working on a dynamo and using visualization but, as he reports, the solution was still in the deep recesses of his brain.

Later, while walking with a friend and reciting Goethe's *Faust,* the idea came to him like a flash of lightning. He drew the diagrams in the sand and later described the incident as a mental state of happiness. Tesla consciously used images. He discovered that by making changes in the images he could isolate the aspects of his work and life that could bring him satisfaction.

Samuels and Samuels (1975), a husband and wife writing team, suggest in *Seeing With the Mind's Eye* that to use images positively, we should locate aspects of life that make us uncomfortable. Through manipulating images, we can discover ways to improve those aspects. They further suggest that when we hold the images in our mind, the images tend to manifest themselves.

Still another famous scientist who tapped his intuition was Rene Descartes. In fact, he has been said to have "rewritten science." In one day of thinking and one night of dreaming, this 23 year old soldier-philosopher reformed the structure of western knowledge by setting down the foundations for a new philosophy, science, and mathematics — a new way of thinking about the world. Jane Muir in *Of Men and Numbers* (1966) reports that Descartes had been applying the method of mathematics to every area of his life. On November 10, 1619, Descartes went to sleep in an overheated room and dreamed three dreams or sleep images that held the key to his search for a new kind of knowledge.

In the first dream, he experienced strong winds blowing him away from a church toward a group of people who weren't affected by the gale. Descartes awoke and then fell asleep again. He heard a bolt of lightning and saw a shower of sparks fill his room. In the third dream, Descartes saw himself holding a dictionary and some papers which contained a poem with the words: "What path shall I follow in life?" An unknown man gave him a verse with the words "Est et Non." At the end of the third dream, he experienced a dream within a dream. He interpreted the dictionary to represent the future unity of science with all the sciences grouped together; the sheaf of poems represented to him the linkage of philosophy and wisdom. "Est et Non" signified truth and falsity in human attainment and in secular sciences.

As a result of this dream, Descartes envisioned himself as the one to reform knowledge and unify the sciences. To him, all of the sciences were interconnected as if by a chain. The dream represents inner knowing and its potential power. He had been involved in a long intense period of preparatory thought, yet the insights did indeed come from a series of images. Science can be conceptualized as a way of looking at the world. Descartes changed that way, and our perspective continues to change from time to time.

E. W. Sinnott (Vernon, 1970), a biologist, describes imagination as a person's ability to picture in the mind's eye something neither seen nor experienced. He stated that the creative process takes place in the unconscious in dreams and half-dreaming states. Sinnott described his mind as filled with images and fantasies. He believed that the unconscious mind rejects certain combinations and selects others as significant. Sinnott makes an analogy between the unconscious mind and what the organism of the brain accomplishes. The organism pulls together random, formless stuff into patterned systems of structure, and functions in the body; the unconscious mind selects, arranges and correlates ideas and images into a pattern.

John Yellot (Hutchinson, 1949), a research engineer studying glass and steam, wrote that he worked hard on a problem without success. Then, while riding on a crowded bus in which he became absorbed in some personal matters, the solution came to him. He described it as a flash and he visualized the drawing of the proper design of the apparatus. He drew it in a notebook and without consciousness of his surroundings wrote down the answer. He also stated that he knew he was right.

Commonalities Among the Scientists and Mathematicians

The images that the scientists report in their moments of illumination have some common characteristics:

A feeling of elation
A feeling of surprise
A sense of the answer appearing as a whole
A sense of the answer as a symbol

Bruner (1973), a Harvard psychologist and educator, lists several conditions for fostering new ideas or inventions. They include detachment and commitment, passion and decorum (respect for the forms and materials that limit one's work), and freedom to be dominated by the object.

Then Bruner suggests deferral and immediacy, an urge to find the problem's solution immediately, but at the same time waiting for the right solution. This last condition has internal drama, in that one is able to become aware of mental figures that personify different aspects within oneself and that approach the problem in different ways. This interchange among the figures produces novel solutions to problems. The stages Bruner suggests are reflected in the work of the scientists that we have examined and are also recognizable in the mathematicians to be discussed in the next section.

Mathematicians and Intuition

The mathematician and philosopher Blaise Pascal said reason is the slow and tortuous method by which those who do not know the truth discover it. To him, intuition had no such restrictions. Intuition was the product of the mind's capacity to accomplish several things simultaneously without being aware of them (Goldberg, 1983).

Ramanujan was born in 1887 to a high caste but poor family in India (Newman, 1948). At an early age he displayed exceptional mathematical skills. When he was fifteen, someone gave him an out-of-date textbook on mathematics which he read and used to construct a massive mathematical knowledge. He told his parents that his ideas and formulas were presented in dreams by the goddess Namagiri. His ability came to the attention of Ramachandra Rao, who then put him in touch with G. H. Hardy, a famous Cambridge mathematician. Hardy, upon examining Ramanujan's work, called him a great mathematician to possess such incredible skill. Hardy secured a scholarship for Ramanujan to study in England. In areas that interested him, Ramanujan was ahead of most contemporary mathematicians, for he had succeeded in recreating over a half-century of European mathematics for himself. How did Ramanujan program himself to know more than he already knew? It was reported that he worked many hours to verify and prove what he often received in an instant, and seldom was his original insight wrong.

A century before Ramanujan, another mathematical prodigy was born to poor parents in Germany. Johann Friedrich Karl Gauss at the age of three interrupted his father to announce that a complicated sum his father was computing was incorrect. His father, according to Hadamard (1949), taught him the alphabet, and Gauss taught himself to read several languages. He mastered classical education as a teenager and decided to major in mathematics. He constructed a seventeen-sided polygon using only a compass and ruler; he reported the solution came to him in a flash. At 23, he discovered the theory of complex numbers. He often described his ideas as coming like a flash of lightning and reported experiencing such a constant stream of ideas that he did not have enough time to complete them.

Still another mathematician of the late nineteenth century was Henri Poincare. Poincare (1924) stated that for fifteen days he tried to prove that there could not be any functions like those he later called Fuchsian functions. Everyday he sat at a work table for an hour or two, tried a great number of combinations and reached no results. One evening, he drank black coffee and could not sleep. That night, ideas rose in crowds; he felt them collide until pairs interlocked, making a stable combination. By the next morning, he had established the existence of a class of Fuchsian functions.

Poincare (1924) cites another example that came to him while stepping onto a bus. He would tackle mathematical mysteries that would obsess him through long conscious labor; then, unexpectedly, the answers would be revealed in moments of insight. Poincare used his own experience as raw data for a detailed analysis of mathematical creativity. In 1908, he published an essay of his work in which he concluded that the appearance of a sudden illumination was a manifest sign of long unconscious work. He felt that exceptional mathematicians are capable of an intuition of mathematical order. He often spoke of the elegance created by mathematical entities whose elements are so harmoniously disposed that the mind effortlessly embraces their totality.

Hutchison (1949) reports another example of insight. He says that Bertrand Russell, a mathematician and philosopher, described his working style as first having a problem or puzzle that he approached with great voluntary application and effort, followed by a period without conscious thought, which often brought a solution.

The Value of Intuition from the Point of View of Scientists

Einstein (1973) stated that there are no logical paths to natural laws: only intuition resting on sympathetic understanding of experience can reach them. Einstein's happiest thought of his life was when he realized that a person falling from a roof was both at rest and in motion at the same time. Einstein said that he discovered the theory of relativity by picturing himself riding on a ray of light. Ghiselin (1952) reports that Einstein wrote to a friend that words did not play a role in his thought. He spoke of psychical entities which seem to serve as elements in thought, as certain signs, and as more or less clear images which can be voluntarily reproduced and combined. John Maynard Keynes said about Isaac Newton that it was his intuition that was preeminently extraordinary (Goldberg, 1983). Newton was happy in his conjectures and had so many that it was impossible to prove all of them. The proofs were dressed up afterwards; they were not the instrument of discovery. What Keynes was reminding us is that the formal proofs were the instruments of verification and communication.

In a sense, many scientists practice intuition. They are presented with hypotheses and they intuitively decide whether they are worth proving. A colleague of ours, who is an inventor, says that intuition helps scientists to know where to look for facts, how to design experiments, and how to interpret data and recognize what is relevant.

The New Age Scientists

Jonas Salk states that it is always with excitement that he awakens in the morning wondering, what his intuition will toss up to him, like gifts from the sea (Goldberg, 1983). Salk works with intuition and relies on it.

A famous supporter of intuition is Apollo 14 astronaut Edgar Mitchell, who left NASA in 1970 and established the Institute of Noetic Sciences. He reported experiencing a state of altered consciousness during his return trip from the moon (Mitchell, 1976). He felt a deep sense of cosmic order and experienced the self-evident ability of the human mind to know itself. Since 1970, Mitchell has devoted his energy to fostering the development of the science of human consciousness.

As the climate of opinion for exploring human consciousness improves, several outstanding ideas and theories have come forth, such as the hologram model for the brain and the holographic model for the universe.

Holographic Brain and Universe

Pribram suggested the hologram as a model for how the brain stores memory (Ferguson, 1980). He said that if memory were distributed rather than localized, it could be holographic. Pribram shared this notion with a friend and took it one step further to suggest that the world might be a hologram. Shortly afterward, he learned of another scientist, a London physicist named Bohm, who was thinking along similar lines.

Bohm was talking and writing about a holographic universe. He wrote that substance and movement were illusory, and that they emerge from another, more primary order called the holomovement.

Holographic theory says that the brain mathematically constructs hard reality by interpreting frequencies from a dimension transcending time and space. In a sense, the brain is a hologram interpreting a holographic universe.

In Bohm's concept of the universe, everything is connected, and time and space are not barriers (Ferguson, 1980). Human consciousness is also part of the plan and, when properly tuned, the human mind can resonate with any portion of it. If the brain works like a hologram storing information in such a way that any piece of information is accessible in its every part, this could explain the rapidity of intuition.

Bohm uses two terms: explicate and implicate. What we normally see is the explicate, or unfolded, order of things. The underlying order is called implicate, or enfolded, which harbors our reality (Ferguson, 1980). Bohm's implicate order is enfolded in the explicate (the familiar world of cause and effect, of separate objects and forms) and constitutes a unified integral whole. As in a hologram, each part of the implicate contains everything in the whole, and the human mind can access that information. Each mind would then contain within it all the information that ever was in the universe (Ferguson, 1980).

This new thinking leads us back to the psychologist Carl Jung (1964) who talked about the collective unconscious where the mind links with a more encompassing field of information and intelligence. According to Jung (1964), individual minds can tap into an information base that is not limited by the restrictions of memory, sense perception, time or space.

New age physicist Fritjof Capra (1975) states in his book *The Tao of Physics* that the universe is engaged in endless motion and activity in a continual cosmic dance of energy. He hypothesizes that subatomic particles are dynamic patterns which do not exist as isolated entities, but as integral parts of an inseparable network of interactions. These interactions involve a ceaseless flow of energy manifesting itself as the exchange of particles. The particle interactions give rise to the stable structures which build up the material world, which again, is not static, but oscillates in rhythmic movement.

Thought, as depicted by these scientists, is helping to explain the intuitive mind. Was the intuitive discovery of the DNA molecule by James Watson a sudden awareness? Obviously Watson and his colleague Francis Crick programmed their intuitive minds with questions, and the solution was an insight into the problem. Or was the information there in the information base to which minds became tuned? This question is very timely considering the work of another scientist, Edward Witten.

A Theory of Everything

Edward Witten of the Institute for Advanced Study was recently interviewed by the *New York Times* (Cole, October 1987) on his applications of physics to mathematics. Witten has started whole groups of people on new paths by calling attention to a long-forgotten theory called "superstring theory." It proposes that the fundamental stuff of nature consists of tiny strings that form vibrating loops. String theory does away with the familiar image of a universe composed of billiard ball-like particles pushed and pulled by familiar forces like gravity and electricity. Quantum theory revealed that the billiard balls had wave-like properties; now, string theory proposes these points are tiny loops or strings which vibrate invisibly in subtle resonances. Witten says these vibrations make up everything in the universe from light to lightning bugs, from gravity to gold. To accept string theory, we must suspend our belief in a world fashioned from the familiar four dimensions of height, breadth, width and time, and substitute six hidden dimensions – for a total of 10.

Witten suggests that we imagine a closed string, a loop of some kind of fundamental stuff. Then imagine that the loop rotates, twists and vibrates, not only in the three familiar spatial dimensions, plus one dimension in time, but also in six other dimensions that we can't perceive. As the loop wriggles, it resonates in many different modes like a ten-dimensional violin string sending out cosmic versions of A or E flat. These vibrations, if string theory is correct, determine all the possible particles and forces of the universe.

Sam Treiman, a member of the physics department at Princeton, states that Witten (a MacArthur fellow and most recently winner of the Alan T. Waterman award for best young researcher) produces elegant breathtaking proofs which people gasp at, leaving them in awe. Witten describes his work style of sitting at a kitchen table, resting his chin on his wrist or lying in bed and thinking. He seldom does calculations except in his mind, and after working the calculations in his mind, he sits down only to calculate a minus sign, or a factor of two. I. M. Singer, a mathematics professor at the Massachusetts Institute of Technology, says that Witten's intuition is fantastic.

Witten describes string theory as a piece of 21st century physics that fell by chance into the 20th century. He represents the new-age breed of physicists and mathematicians that are asking us to leap into a world of infinite dimension.

Carl Jung (1971) theorizes that the self sends images to the ego and that images sent by the self are those most necessary to a person's inner growth and development. He suggests images are self-regulatory, and help us develop and grow. Jung states that images are at the center of the universe, and when common images are held by many people, they can solve a common cultural problem. In Jung's (1933) *Modern Man in Search of a Soul,* he said that images are the homeostatic mechanism of the universe, and when images that we hold in our mind are manifested in the outer world, each person becomes a creator. Visualizing is the mechanism of creation. In a sense, visualization becomes reality, and reality is a reflection of our internal images. Scientists, notably physicists, are beginning to agree that each person has far greater power than was conceptualized in the past. Each person can be said to have the power to change the world if the inner and outer become one.

The beckoning from the field of science and to all of us is aptly captured by Guillaume Appollinaire:

> *Come to the edge, he said.*
> *They said: We are afraid.*
> *Come to the edge, he said.*
> *They came.*
> *He pushed them . . . and they flew.*

References

Bohm, D. (1980). *Wholism and the implicate order.* London, England: Routledge & Kegan.
Bohr, N. (1934). *Atomic physics and the description of nature.* Cambridge, MA: Cambridge University Press.
Bruner, J. (1973). *Beyond the information given.* NY: Norton.
Bruner, J. & Clinchy, B. (1971). In J. Bruner (Ed.). *Toward a disciplined intuition in the relevance of education.* NY: Norton.
Capra, F. (1975). *The tao of physics.* Berkeley, CA: Shambhala.
Cole, K. C. (1987). A theory of everything. *The New York Times Magazine,* October 18, 20-28.
Einstein, A. (1973). *Ideas and opinions.* NY: Dell.
Einstein, A. & Infeld, L. (1938). *The evolution of physics.* NY: Simon & Shuster.

Ferguson, M. (1980). *The aquarian conspiracy.* Los Angeles, CA: Jeremy P. Tarcher, Inc.
Ghiselin, B. (1952). *The creative process.* NY: New American Library.
Goldberg, P. (1983). *The intuitive edge.* Los Angeles, CA: Jeremy R. Tarcher, Inc.
Hadamard, J. (1949). *The psychology of invention in the mathematical field.* Princeton, NJ: Princeton University Press.
Harman, W. & Rheingold, H. (1984). *Higher creativity: Liberating the consciousness for breakthrough insights.* Los Angeles, CA: Jeremy R. Tarcher, Inc.
Hutchinson, E. (1949). *How to think creatively.* NY: Abingdon-Cokesberry.
Jung, C. G. (1933). *Modern man in search of a soul.* NY: Harcourt Brace & World.
Jung, C. G. (1964). *Man and his symbols.* Garden City, NY: Doubleday.
Jung, C. G. (1971). *Psychological types.* Princeton, NJ: Princeton University Press.
Kaempffert, W. B. (1924). *A popular history of American invention* (Vol. II). NY: Charles Scribner & Sons.
Kedrov, B. M. (1957). On the question of scientific creativity. *Voprosy Psychology, 3,* 91-113.
Loewi, O. (1960). An autobiographical sketch. *Perspectives in Biology and Medicine,* Autumn.
Mitchell, E. (1976). In J. White (Ed.). *From outer space to inner space.* NY: Putnam.
Muir, J. (1966). *Of men and numbers.* NY: Dodd & Mead.
Newman, J. (1948). Srinavas Ramanujan. *Scientific American, 178* (6), 54-57.
Poincaire, H. (1924). Mathematical creation. In G. B. Halstead (Ed.), *The Foundations of Sciences.* NY: The Science Press.
Pribram, K. (1971). *Languages of the brain.* Englewood Cliffs, NJ: Prentice Hall.
Samuels, M. & Samuels, N. (1975). *Seeing with the mind's eye.* NY: Random House.
Sorokin, P. (1965). *A systematic sourcebook in rural sociology.* NY: Russell & Russell.
Talamundi, L. (1975). *Forbidden universe.* NY: Stein & Day.
Tesla, N. (1919). My inventions. *Electrical Experimentor,* May.
Vernon, P. E. (1970). *Creativity: Selected readings.* NY: Penguin Books.

CHAPTER EIGHT

The Myth of Women's Intuition

Women hold up half of the sky.

Chinese Proverb

For years we have talked in generalities about the masculine and feminine sides of our natures. Independence and intellect have been thought to be masculine, while nurturance and intuition have been considered feminine. This latter generalization has been perpetuated as the myth of women's intuition. When did this myth begin? The answer lies in the examination of the history of creation and creation goddesses searching for universal themes and symbols; in the ancient arts of healing and forecasting that were women's responsibilities, and in tracing the rise of patriarchy and the suppression of women and their powers. Two examples of women who have responded to deep intuition are evidence of the potential that can be enjoyed by intuition, and the challenge for the future for both men and women.

Through the years women have had cultural permission to be more intuitive, nurturing, sensitive and feeling. Many of these characteristics are skills from the ancient times when women were the caregivers. Anne Fausto-Sterling (1985) in her book *Myths of Gender* begins one chapter with two quotes that pose two definite points of view at two separate points in time (one by Steven Goldberg (1973), and another by John Stuart Mill in 1873):

> We are assuming... that there are no differences between men and women except on the hormonal level system that renders the man more aggressive. This alone would explain patriarchy, male dominance, and male attainment of high status roles, for the male hormonal system gives men an insuperable head start (Steven Goldberg, 1973).

> Of all the vulgar modes of escaping from the consideration of the effect of social and moral influences upon the human mind, the most vulgar is that of attributing the diversities of conduct and character to inherent natural differences (John Stuart Mill, 1806-1873).

Fausto-Sterling's book examines any number of myths of gender, an example of which is the question of lateralization. She reports that there is no solid evidence for the idea that females are more bilateral than males in verbal functioning, but that there does seem to be evidence that females use their left hemisphere (their verbal hemisphere) more frequently to solve visual-spatial problems. However, this does not necessarily imply a sex-related difference, but could reflect different problem-solving strategies. She reports that, for whatever reasons, females prefer to use verbal approaches to the solution of spatial problems.

Sherman (1977) suggests the bent twig hypothesis, in which girls are hypothesized to develop their language ability earlier than boys do, thereby beginning a chain of reactions that give females progressively greater language skills. As girls talk earlier, parents may talk more with their daughters and further develop their daughters' language skills. Because of their skill, girls may choose verbal mediation over so called Gestalt processes for the solution of visual-spatial problems. So, even though Sherman and other researchers believe that early verbal development in girls is biological, it may well be environmental interaction as well.

The cultural environment for women is evolving today and historical review indicates a dramatic change from an ancient matriarchal society to a patriarchy with some vestiges still existing in the 1980s.

Creation and Creation Goddesses

Creation is defined as a starting action or point from which all life and accomplishment take place. It is bringing order out of disorder and a beginning that becomes fulfillment. According to Stein (1987), creation in every ancient culture is a female act. She reports that, before the patriarchal era, people described the beginnings of the universe in terms of the female giving birth and life. From Pre-Hellenic Greece to the Native American Hopi, from Africa to the Near East and South America, the stories all have a similar strand. First there was nothingness that became chaos. Chaos is defined as all things in infinite potential, but without form or order, the watery abyss of the universe. Chaos is a female fertility concept associated with the moon and the evolving sea of earth. The creator of this teeming abyss was sometimes called Gaia, Yernaya, Spider Woman, Ishatar or Ashtoreth. She rose from chaos and ordered it into form, putting things in their place and birthing planets, people and all of life. Noble (1983) reports:

> The Goddess of all things rose naked from chaos and found nowhere to place her foot. Separating the sea from the sky, she brooded over the waters until she gave birth to life: Herself.

This goddess, according to Noble, is always the moon, and her body is also the earth that she creates, the land and seas, with all that live there being nourished from her and returning to her at death. She shines in the universe above, waxing and waning in her cycles. In alter ages, she is given a consort, male or female, but born from the goddess parthenogentically as her daughter, companion, or mates. The stories of Ashtoreth and Baal, Ishatar and Tammuz are examples and reflect the process of creation in the changing cycles of the year.

There are many goddess creation stories, yet they have one thing in common in that they all tell how the world came to be in female and natural order terms and use symbols of the birthing of life. The oldest pre-Hellenic goddess is Gaia who arose from herself, from chaos.

Gaia

Whirling in darkness, Gaia became a galaxy of fiery light and created the sun and the moon, the mirror of heaven. Merging with heaven, herself in the mirror, she gave birth to seas and, after cooling, became the planet. Gaia's body was the mother, the female, the fertile earth. She was Gaia the all-giver, all-mother and Pandora. Spretnak (1981) reports in her book *Lost Goddesses of Early Greece* that Gaia gave birth to six women and six men, the goddesses and gods. All came to Gaia to her wisdom and she granted the gift of prophecy to those who

asked through her priestesses (Stein, 1987; Gonzales-Wippler, 1981).
By the time of classical Greece, the stories include Gaia as the creator of a universe born of herself and birthing a son by parthenogenesis, Uranus who was heaven to her earth. Eventually Gaia was depicted as Hera, the nagging wife of Zeus.

Yemaya

The goddess creation story is known throughout West Africa and South and Central America by several names including Umoja, Ymoja, Yamanza, Iamanza, and the Yoruban mermaid goddess Yemaya. Yemaya is a moon goddess of waters and oceans. She births the children of the world. Gonzales-Wippler reports in 1981 that in Cuba and Brazil the goddess is described as yellowish in skin, and beautiful.

In the Yoruban Genesis story, when the immortal first man's conceit caused the gods to destroy all life, Olodumare (creation) felt sorry and created a new mortal god-human, Obtala. Obtala was given a wife, Oddudua, who was portrayed as a young black woman breastfeeding a child. The children of Obatala and Oddudua were Aganyu and Yamaya. Yamaya was raped by her son and she cursed him, and died of sorrow. At her death, her womb opened and the birth waters caused a great flood; from her bones were born Obafulom and Lyaa, the first human man and woman, parents of the people (Gonzalez-Wippler, 1981). Yamaya is an image of fertile birth and creativity of all sorts, of the life-giving, life-emerging waters. She is imaged as the moon and is a women's diety, a goddess of mercy.

Spider Woman

The goddess counterpart in southwest North America is Spider Woman, the weaver of life, great mother of the Hopi Indians. Spider Woman arose from nothingness at the time of the dark purple light before dawn. She spun a silver strand to connect the east and the west of the horizon and then spun another strand from north to south with herself as the center.

Waters (1963) in his *Book of the Hopi* reports that Spider Woman:

> created from the earth, trees, bushes, plants and flowers, all kinds of seed bearers and nut bearers to clothe the earth, giving to each a life and a name. In the same manner, she created all kinds of birds and animals – molding them out of earth.

Spider Woman created the four colors of people (red, yellow, black and white) from the four colors of clay and spun life from her body. When the people awoke, they were connected by a spider filament at the *kopavi*, the purple light *chakra* at the crown of their heads. Spider Woman told them to keep this door open to her, to creation, spirituality and the life force.

Ishatar

The goddess Ishatar of Ashtore was another creation figure and great mother (Harding, 1971). She was a goddess whose far reaching influence has shaped world cultures, world religions and civilizations. Her origins were Babylonian, and her worship extended through the Near East. She was the prototype for Isis, the Egyptian great mother goddess, as well as the Greek Aphrodite or Venus. Her Canaanite forms, Ashtoreth, Asherah, Astarte or Anat were the matriarchal origins of the Hebrew Yahweh. Ashtoreth's story is similar to that of Inanna, the Sumerian goddess. Ashtoreth is depicted as a serpent goddess, her body entwined with snakes and bearing the lunar disc and crescent horns upon her head. She is called Serpent Lady and Ashtorth of the Horns of the Queen of Heaven. Ishtar is named as creator of the universe and is the goddess of fertility and affirms life – including plant, animal and human. She created the universe from chaos, but was lonely. By parthenogenesis she gave birth to a son, Tammuz or Baal, Adonis or Damuzi.

Reverence for Women

Each of the creation goddesses – Gaia, Yamaya, Spider Woman, and Ishtar – created the earth by birth or created all life by shaping. They were the earth and moon in one. Their symbols and legends were examples of worldwide stories and depict the goddess as the creative force of the universe.

Before the institutional Protestant or Catholic churches, before Judaism, before Islam or classical Greece, before there was God or gods, there was the goddess in every culture and civilization. Women were reverenced as a birth-giving image. Each culture had its creation and power story, and reverence for the life force carried over into reverence for women.

As civilization moved from food gatherers and men became hunters, the female who gives and takes all in equal abundance was no longer enough of an image. Diner (1973) reports that the concept of a hunter god began, first as a consort to the goddess, but increasingly superseding her:

> Slowly the powers of the gods underwent a transition. At first the male appeared only as an adjunct to the great Mother. Later he became the lord of storms and the moon.

Universal Symbols

Symbols of all creative goddesses are universals that surround human consciousness, such as sea and sea creatures, eggs, woven mazes, or labyrinth spirals, circles and triangles, and the self-renewing serpent. Merlin Stone (1984) in her book *Ancient Mirrors of Womanhood* states that life came from the sea and all that is of oceans are the lunar goddess. She reports that many cultures depict the great mother as a mermaid, including the Yoruban Yamaya, Tiamat of Babylonia, Atargatis of Syria and the Sumerian goddesses Nina and Nidaba, Nu Kwa of China and the Japanese Kwannon.

Fish are associated with any sea goddess and this symbol was later adapted into Christianity. These similarities found in many cultures with widespread geographies are intriguing. The symbols were transformed under patriarchy from benevolent life symbols to the downfall of Eve. As patriarchy gained strength, the goddess of the moon became a monster to be slain by men. Snakes that had been goddess symbols for their self-renewing shedding became loathed and feared. Just as Saint George slew the dragon, the forces of matriarchy and goddess religion were slain in the Christianizing of Europe.

Other symbols are reported by Cooper (1982) such as shells, pearls and fishes that depict life and evolving life. The conch sound of the sea is believed in India to be the sound that made the universe. Stein (1987) reminds us that Aphrodite in Greece was sea-born, that Teteu Innan, an Aztec goddess, wears a seashell skirt, and that the Navahos have a white shell woman.

Rise of Patriarchy

As the male god supplanted the female aspect, the split between the dualities of male and female, death and birth, earth and universe, and the change from the goddess to patriarchy was accomplished. The goddess became Yahweh, the jealous male god of the desert Jews. Worship of Ashtoreth, Tammuz or Baal was attacked in the Old Testament . . .

*And I will put an end to all her mirth
her feasts, her new moons, her sabbaths . . .
And I will punish her for the feast days of the Ba'als
when she burned incense to them.*

Hosea 2

As patriarchy assumed strength, references to feasts and goddess worship were being ended by Judaism. In early Jewish folklore, Lilith was the first woman made of earth as Adam was the first man. However, when Lilith refused to be subordinated by Adam, she left Eden and became a monster to frighten children. To maintain the male power of the early Hebrew God, goddess worship had to be uprooted. Women were refused education and any form of leadership or authority. Orthodox Judaism said that women had no soul and, by the time of Christianity, women were able to own nothing.

As Christianity grew from a small cult to a world institution, it also grew in its anti-goddess/anti-woman convictions. Women were to be silent and subservient, own nothing in the law and be ruled by their husbands. Men were believed to be the new images of God and his Son. Through the conquering of matriarchy, through centuries of Judaism and the rise of Christianity, through the agony of the Inquisition in which the word for female, "femina," was said to mean lack of faith, women were viewed as the source of world evil.

Yet, in the past women had been the healers and the life givers. Today many women are re-claiming, re-visioning, and discovering what their spirituality is all about.

Women as Healers and Forecasters

Women from ancient times have been healers. The knowledge of healing in the use of herbs, colors, aura work, reflexology, midwifery, massage, crystals and trance states have been part of the history of women. Healing in the matriarchy was women's work connected to birth, death and the life force.

Healing knowledge went underground during the patriarchy, but it did survive. Today, many of the traditional techniques and skills are being reclaimed and relearned. Herbal medicine was early a women's field, with Hildegarde of Bingen's twelfth-century work still considered classic. However, most of the skills of healing and forecasting were handed down by oral tradition.

Reflexology involves the relief of pain by stimulation of mapped nerve centers that relate to organs and glands of the body. A type of massage, used with reflexology, includes full body work that uses touch, stroking and kneading. It stimulates muscles, skin and energy centers to increase circulation, release blockages and pain, shape body tone and invoke deep relaxation. Inherent in all of the healing skills is caring. The trance states of deep relaxation and creative visualization, of color work and auras are basic to psychic healing. Colors are used in meditation and in healing. A violet light bulb shining as the only light (according to Ouseley [1949] in *Colour Meditation*) can overcome sleeplessness. A green light is antiseptic in cases of infection, and a blue colored light can be used to reduce swelling (fifteen minutes on the exact area to be healed). Yellow light can be used for exhaustion as it activates the solar plexus.

Color can also be used for mood altering. Red, orange and yellow are hot and arousing; green is soothing; blue, indigo and violet are sedating. For lethargy, we can use red or orange; for nervousness and stress, use violet.

Stein (1987) in the *Women's Spirituality Book* suggests that creative visualization be used in harmony with healing. She suggests that you enter the trance state by deep breathing and full body relaxation and visualize white light. See as completely as possible the person to be healed. Visualize using white light through your hands to fill in the person's aura with color, or use a specific healing color. Stein suggests channeling the energy from the earth or sky, and return it to the sky or earth when it leaves the person who is to be healed. See the person as being totally well, and see an aura of full energy, beauty, health and peace.

Crystals are also used in connection with healing since they magnify, store and focus energy and are used to transmit and direct energy. Crystals can focus and clarify dreams. Da El (1983) in the *Crystal Power* classifies crystal attributes into amplification and clarity, transforming, storage of information and energy, focusing, energy transferring, and altered states of consciousness. Da El suggests picking a crystal by attraction. Touch it and hold it in your left hand. Look for a stone that resonates with your individual aura. It will feel alive in your hand. It will vibrate and radiate. Clear quartz is the stone with the most power.

With your new crystal in your hand, clear your mind and hold your crystal to make it your own. Bond with it. Feel its vibrations, colors and sounds. Visualize colors flowing through the crystal. If you are feeling cool or chilled, hold your crystal in the left hand and feel warmth. For cheering, draw yellow in and for calming, draw blue or indigo in. Focus on your breathing and at the count of 1-2-3 be aware of your everyday surroundings.

Gemstones can also be used for healing. Amethyst is violet in color and corresponds to the crown chakra, the violet color band in the spiritual aura. Amethyst can be used for calming, grounding and balancing. The moonstone heightens psychic sensitivity and trance states. The blue saphire can be used for insight and perception and corresponds to the brow chakra. McBride et al. (1982) call the saphire the supreme gem. It raises vibrations to spiritual levels and induces positive self-image. The lapis lazuli is a stone for the throat chakra and was the healer's stone in ancient Egypt (for the sky goddess Nuit), and of Isis. The lapis opens the chakas and strengthens and balances psychic experiences. Emerald is a heart chakra and draws beauty and love. Carnelian and red coral open the belly chakra, the color orange. Yellow stones such as amber or topaz open the solar plexus chakra. Garnets open the root chakra and offer courage, constancy and endurance.

Visualization (as discussed in other chapters) is the heart of most of the healing and forecasting skills. It leads to altered states in which questions can be drawn into the visualization and be answered.

An eastern technique that has been modified is to visualize the image of the goddess herself. See her as a mermaid, a serpent, a woman. See her as dark-skinned or light, blonde or Afro-haired. See her speaking in all languages. Ask her a question, or what she wills, and see yourself receiving an answer. See yourself sending inner light from your heart chakra to the visualization of the goddess. This light surrounds the goddess with love and light. Draw the image into your own heart. See the goddess within you and at the count of 1-2-3 return to your present day awareness. This visualization is modified from Diane Mariechild's *Mother Wit: A Feminist Guide to Psychic Development* (1981). People who use these guided stories or visualizations report feelings of peace and love and insight coming into their lives. The ability to use visualization is a skill that gains in power with practice.

Personal Illumination

Maslow, in his book *Religions, Values and Peak Experiences,* reminds us that at the very beginning, the intrinsic core, the essence, or the universal nucleus of every known high religion is the private, lonely, personal illumination, revelation or ecstasy of some acutely sensitive person. Two women fall into that category. One is Jane Roberts who has become one of the twentieth century's most famous channels to another personality called Seth. In over 1000 sessions of taped or transcribed sessions with Seth, a central theme is introduced, that of the importance of personal, societal and global belief systems. Seth talks about how personal beliefs can and do affect the way we perceive and the way we live.

Jane Roberts (1972) was interested in extrasensory perception and, in her experiments with a Ouija board, Seth emerged. Seth answers the skeptics by saying:

> If the universe existed as you have been told it does, then I would not be writing this book. There would be no psychological avenues to connect my world and yours.

Still another personal illumination is that of Dr. Helen Schucman, a psychologist on the staff of Presbyterian Hospital at Columbia University. As both a psychologist and educator, she was surprised when a kind of rapid inner dictation began taking place within her, accompanied by strange images. After 1500 pages of manuscript had been dictated, Schucman took the material to a colleague, Dr. William Thetfore, who was also on the staff at Presbyterian Hospital. Together they decided to use the material in their personal lives, but to keep it a secret from their colleagues. They feared intellectual criticism and rejection.

For five years, the document was hidden until, one day during a luncheon, Judith Skutch (an individual active in parapsychology and research) indicated her interest in inner voices. This led Schucman and Thetford to share the document. The course now known as *Miracles* consists of 365 psychospiritual exercises based on the power of affirmation and provides a way for the reader to find their own internal teacher. The underlying principle or theme of the course is the same as that of Seth's: that internal beliefs create what is perceived as reality and we are imprisoned by the cage of our wrong beliefs. These old beliefs can be replaced by affirming new beliefs. The course affirms that there is a part of ourself that knows the way to health, wholeness and success, referred to as the "still small voice within."

Harman and Rheingold (1984) report that, since publication *of miracles,* scientists, lawyers, foundation heads, businessmen, psychologists, and housewives have used the exercises. They report resulting loss of anxiety, fear, depression and guilt, a feeling of deep connection with the universe, and feelings of peace and love. These two women are extraordinary examples of deep intuition and they amplify by example the notion that the spectrum of human creativity is multidimensional.

Challenge for the Future

Perhaps by exploring the history of women's spirituality and the early reverence of women, and by pondering examples of deep intuition, we can become more in tune with expecting the unexpected. By being true to the integrity of the moment, there is reason to believe that intuition as discussed in this chapter can become a knowledge for all of us. Over the years, we have progressed from goddess worship to a patriarchy that suppressed women. Yet somehow, there has been a subtle cultural permission for women to be more intuitive, more sensitive, more feeling. Today's challenge is for women and men together to create a new future.

Ferguson (1980) reports that Lou Harris of the Harris Poll said that women are far ahead of men in pushing for basic human qualities. He found that they were more dedicated to peace and opposed to war, more concerned over child abuse, and deeply moved by what he called the pall of violence.

Women can bring special qualities to this new society that can be created by women and men together. With emphasis on women's qualities that are necessary to change life and create a sustaining relationship with the universe — such as integration, empathy, reconciliation and greater sensitivity to time and season, intuition about direction and ability to wait — the future may well belong to women *and* men in harmony.

References

Cooper, J. C. (1982). *Symbolism, the universal language.* Aquarian Press.
Da El. (1983). *The crystal book.* Sunol, CA: The Crystal Company.
Diner, H. (1973). *Mothers and amazons: The first feminine history of culture.* NY: Anchor Books.
Fausto-Sterling, A. (1985). *Myths of gender.* NY: Basic Books.
Ferguson, M. (1980). *The aquarian conspiracy.* Los Angeles, CA: Jeremy P. Tarcher, Inc.
Gonzales-Wippler, M. (1981). *Santeria: African magic in Latin America.* NY: Original Products Inc.
Harding, E. (1971). *Women's mysteries: Ancient and modern.* San Francisco, CA: Harper & Row.

Harman, W. & Rheingold, H. (1984). *Higher creativity: Liberating the unconscious for breakthrough insights.* Los Angeles, CA: Jeremy P. Tarcher, Inc.
Jung, C. G. (1973). *Jung, synchronicity, and human destiny.* NY: Julian Press.
Mariechild, D. (1981). *Mother wit: A feminist guide to psychic development.* Freedom, CA: Crossing Press.
Maslow, A. (1976). *Religions, values and peak experiences.* NY: Penguin Books.
McBride, R., Devery, L., Deering, C. & Amber, K. (1982). Occult uses of gemstones. *Circle Network News,* Summer, 12.
Noble, A. (1983). *Motherpeace: A way to the goddess through myth, art and tarot.* San Francisco, CA: Harper & Row.
Ouseley, S. G. J. (1949). *Colour meditations, with guide to colour healing.* L. N. Fowler & Co.
Roberts, J. (1972). *Seth speaks.* NY: Bantam Books.
Roberts, J. (1974). *The nature of personal reality.* Englewood Cliffs, CA: Prentice-Hall.
Sherman, J. (1977). Effects of biological factors on sex-related differences in mathematics. *NIE Paper,* Washington, DC: Institute of Education.
Spretnak, C. (1981). *Lost goddesses of early Greece.* Boston, MA: Beacon Press.
Stein, D. (1987). *The women's spirituality book.* St. Paul, MN: Llewellyn New Times.
Waters, F. (1963). *Book of the Hopi.* NY: Ballantine Books.

CHAPTER NINE

Spirituality and Intuition

When the pupil is ready, the teacher will come.

Chinese Proverb

The kind of intuitive experience which leads most directly to a sense of well-being and harmony with oneself and the universe is the mystical or transpersonal experience. In both Eastern and Western spiritual traditions, intuitive knowledge is recognized as the highest form of truth. This truth, this Ultimate Reality, this Absolute Being, this Source and Ground of all that is, is often conceived in personal terms and called God. Mystics believe that there is an Ultimate Being, a dimension of existence beyond that experienced through the sense. The Upanishads (ancient Indian doctrine) say, *"The Atman (godhead) is that by which the universe is pervaded."*

What this condition, state, phenomenon, this level of consciousness, this form of cosmic consciousness — called by so many different names — does afford a person is the immediate knowledge of a reality underlying the physical world. Harman and Rheingold (1987) in *Higher Creativity* quote Michael Murphy, one of the founders of the Esalen Institute in California, an organization devoted to exploring human potential and bringing together the world's great spiritual teachers and leaders. Murphy states: *"The central perception . . . is that there is a fundamental reality, godhead, or ground of existence that transcends the ordinary world, yet exists in it."*

At the core of the esoteric beliefs systems, according to Murphy, is the idea that *"The spiritual reality that is the source of all consciousness can be known."* This is what Rufus Jones, in *The Encyclopedia of Religion and Ethics*, called *"the type of religion which puts the emphasis on direct and immediate consciousness of the Divine Presence,"* and this is what St. Thomas Aquinas meant when he spoke of the knowledge of God through experience.

Perhaps a differentiation that Roberto Assagioli makes in Psychosynthesis in regard to how religion can be, and has been, considered at two different stages would be helpful:

1. The "existential religious or spiritual experience," that is, the direct experience of spiritual realities. This stage has been realized by the founders of religions, the mystics, some philosophers and, in varying degrees, by many people.
2. The theological or metaphysical *formulations* of such experiences and the *institutions* which have been founded, in various historical periods and "cultural spaces," in order to communicate its fruits and outcomes to the masses of men who did not have that direct experience. Further, the *methods, forms* and *rites* through which the masses of men may be helped to participate – indirectly – in the revelation (Assagioli, 1965).

Some people, then, become followers of those whose direct experience has served as an inspiration. They follow paths, rituals, and the like, which have been established – i.e., prayer, meditation – aspiring to (and possibly attaining) their own direct experiences.

When we speak of "direct experience," such as Thomas Aquinas' knowledge of God through experience, we mean one's ability to make a spiritual connection – forming a union with God or Ultimate Reality – attaining satori, nirvana, cosmic consciousness or Self-Realization, or all the Self is and can be beyond the limiting ego status. (Self is capitalized to distinguish it from the individual self – the ego of changing personality with which we normally identify. Thus, in the state of transcendence, what is illumined is one's ultimate identity. We come to know that which we are [Goldberg, 1983].)

Direct experience, an inner way of knowing, is different from the ordinary experience of knowing. The ordinary way always has two components: a subject (the experience) and an object of experience. There is a separation between the knower and what is known. This separation is often referred to as a duality which needs to be overcome if one is to experience a true spiritual union. That is what is meant by the concept of achieving oneness with the universe. Astronaut Edgar Mitchell said:

> It is becoming increasingly clear that the human mind and the physical universe do not exist independently. Something as yet undefinable connects them. This connective link — between mind and matter, intelligence and intuition — is what Noetic Sciences is all about.

The purpose of the Noetics institute is to expand knowledge of the nature and potentials of the mind and spirit, and to apply that knowledge to the advancement of health and well-being for humankind. Mitchell chose the word Noetic — from the Greek "nous" meaning mind, intelligence, understanding — to encompass the diverse ways of knowing: the reasoning processes of the intellect, the perceptions of our physical senses, and the intuitive, spiritual or inner ways of knowing.

Spiritual intuition as a holistic perception of reality transcends rational, dualistic ways of knowing and gives the individual a direct transpersonal experience of the underlying oneness of life, says Frances Vaughan (1979). Vaughan reports on Abraham Maslow's study of self-actualizing persons:

> While this transcendence of dichotomy can be seen as a usual thing in self-actualizing persons, it can also be seen in most of people in their most acute moments of integration with the self and between the self and the world. In the highest love between man and woman, parent and child, as the people reach the ultimates of strength, self-esteem, or individuality, so also do they simultaneously merge with the other, lose self-consciousness and more or less transcend the self and selfishness.

Maslow, then, categorizes one type of his "peak experiences" as transcending dualistic modes of knowing (rational, conceptual) and utilizing non-dualistic modes of knowing (intuitive, holistic).

Mentioned previously was the idea of spiritual intuition as a level of consciousness. It is referred to as "pure consciousness," that is, spiritual intuition is distinguished from other forms by its independence from sensations, feelings and thoughts. Goldberg (1983) says that in transcendence, the experience is conscious, but not conscious *of* anything; awareness alone exists. The knower knows but there is no object of knowledge; knowingness alone exists. Goldberg offers a good analogy:

> It is as if the film in a movie projector has run out but the projector light remains on, illuminating the screen. Previously, the viewer's attention had been on the changing forms and colors that to him constituted reality. Now he is aware of the screen itself, the silent, formless background on which the variegated experiences depend. In Transcendence, the silent backdrop to experience is illuminated. This is pure consciousness.

Abraham Maslow in 1969 coined the term Transpersonal Psychology to identify an emerging extension of psychological inquiry. Transpersonal Psychology investigates the evolution of consciousness and experiences which lie beyond the person, including the highest visions, goals and aspirations of human beings. The Institute of Transpersonal Psychology in Menlo Park, California describes the discipline in this way: Transpersonal Psychology integrates knowledge and insights from Western, as well as Eastern, psychological and spiritual approaches. It recognizes and studies the place of unity at the core of every spiritual tradition and seeks to apply these insights to gain new perspectives in fostering human growth and creativity and in dealing effectively with the challenges of today.

Transpersonal education is derived from this branch of psychology. In transpersonal education, the learner is encouraged to be awake and autonomous, to question, to explore all the corners and crevices of conscious experience, to seek meaning, to test outer limits, and to check out frontiers and depths of the self. Marilyn Ferguson (1980) in *The Aquarian Conspiracy* states:

> In contrast to conventional education, which aims to adjust the individual to society as it exists, the "humanistic" educators of the 1960s maintained that the society should accept its members as unique and autonomous. Transpersonal experience aims for a new kind of learner and a new kind of society. Beyond self-acceptance, it promotes self-transcendence.

Ferguson feels that transpersonal education aids the learner's search for meaning, the need to discuss forms and patterns, and the hunger for harmony. It deepens awareness of how a paradigm shifts, or how frustration and struggle precede insights. Among a number of comparisons between what she calls the old paradigm of education and the new paradigm of learning that seem especially to speak to the need for transpersonal education are these:

Assumptions of the Old Paradigms of Education	Assumptions of the New Paradigms of Learning
Emphasis on *content,* acquiring a body of "right" information once and for all.	Emphasis on learning how to learn, how to ask good questions, paying attention to the right things, being open to and evaluating new concepts, and having access to information. What is now "known" may change. Importance of *context.*
Learning as a *product,* a destination.	Learning as a *process,* a journey.
Emphasis on external world. Inner experience often considered inappropriate in school setting.	Inner experience, seen as context for learning. Use of dream journals, imagery, storytelling, centering exercises, and exploraiton of feelings encouraged.
Emphasis on analytical, linear, left-brain thinking.	Strives for whole-brain education. Augments left-brain rationality with holistic, non-linear, and intuitive strategies. Confluence and fusion of the two processes emphasized.
Concern with norms.	Concern with the individual's performance in terms of potential. Interest in testing outer limits, transcending perceived limitations.

Abraham Maslow, in his hierarchy of human needs, spoke of the highest level, the fifth level, as self-actualization. Just prior to his death in 1970, he added the sixth level that could go beyond self-actualization into a state referred to as "transcendence." Maslow felt this to be the level of interconnectedness, the state of oneness with the universe that would include and use all of human functioning at its highest actualization. Today, transpersonal education is beginning to take hold, and the thoughts of East and West are coming together in a climate of acceptance.

Until the last few decades, Eastern philosophies and religions received little attention in the Western world. Generally, spiritual and religious interest in intuition is divided into two categories: philosophies and religions with a primarily Eastern focus, and those which reflect a more Western, or Judeo-Christian, influence. The Judeo-Christian tradition has typically not been as intuitively oriented as the philosophies and religions of the East (Noddings & Shore, 1984). When intuitive experiences have been recognized and sanctioned by Christian churches, they have usually taken the more passive form of revelation, in which the knower receives the knowledge. Noddings and Shore point out that the Christian intuiter may feel at one with God or the cosmos, but in a subordinate way that differs dramatically from the Zen or Hindu intuitive experience. They single out Alan Watts as one of the modern philosophers and writers who recognized these limitations on the Christian notion of intuition and attempted to integrate more intuitive ways of knowing with Christian beliefs. Watts' (1962) book, *The Joyous Cosmology: Adventures in the Chemistry of Consciousness,* can be helpful to those interested in delving deeper into these modern Western thoughts on spirituality and consciousness.

Although most Eastern religions concern themselves with intuitive ways of knowing, the two Eastern philosophies which seem to have had the greatest impact on the Western world are Zen Buddhism and Taoism. It is presumptuous to describe these philosophies briefly, but perhaps enough of their essence will come through for those unfamiliar with them.

Zen Buddhism is a unique blend of the philosophies and idiosyncrasies of three different cultures. First, it is derived from Indian thought in the form of Buddhism. Then it went through the Chinese Ch'an philosophy (around A.D. 100) which concentrated on Buddhism's practical aspects and developed them into a special kind of spiritual discipline. This Ch'an philosophy was eventually adopted by Japan (around A.D. 1200) and has been cultivated in Japan under the name of Zen, which is a tradition still practical there.

D. T. Suzuki (1964) states that Zen discipline is enlightenment. The attainment of enlightenment is an experience known as *satori*. All Eastern philosophies have as their essence the enlightenment experience, but Zen is unique in that it concentrates exclusively on this experience and does not concern itself with the rest of Buddhist doctrine.

According to Fritjof Capra (1975). Zen has no special doctrine or philosophy and no formal creeds or dogmas. Zen asserts that this freedom from all fixed beliefs makes it truly spiritual. More than any other school of Eastern Mysticism, Zen is convinced that words can never express the ultimate truth. Yet, as Capra states, the Zen experience can be passed on from teacher to pupil, and it has, in fact, been transmitted for many centuries by special methods proper to Zen. In a classic summary of four lives, Zen is described as:

> A special transmission outside the scriptures, not founded upon words and letters, pointing directly to the human mind, seeing into one's nature and attaining Buddhahood.

Capra remarks that this technique of "direct pointing" constitutes the special flavor of Zen. It is typical of the Japanese mind (which is more intuitive than intellectual) and likes to give out facts as facts without much comment. Zen does not deal at all with theorizing, conceptualizing, speculation, or abstract thinking. Enlightenment in Zen means active participation in everyday affairs. The masters say that Zen is our daily experience, the everyday mind. Their emphasis is on awakening in the midst of everyday affairs; they made it clear that they saw everyday life not only as the way to enlightenment, but as enlightenment itself. In Zen, *satori* means the immediate experience of the Buddha nature of all things. The perfection of Zen is to live one's everyday life naturally and spontaneously. Capra states Zen is the belief in the perfection of our original nature, and the realization that the process of enlightenment consists merely in becoming what we already are from the beginning.

Of the two main Chinese trends of thought — Confucianism and Taoism — Taoism is more mystically oriented and is interested in intuitive wisdom rather than in rational knowledge. Mistrust of conventional knowledge and reason is stronger in Taoism than in any other school of Eastern philosophy. Tao (the Way) means *seeing* which in turn means *intuition*. In his exemplary book, *The Tao of Physics*, Fritjof Capra (1976) points out that Taoists consider logical reasoning as part of the artificial world of man. They concentrate their full attention on the observation of nature in order to discern the "characteristics of the Tao." They develop an attitude that is essentially scientific; only their deep mistrust in the analytic method prevents them from constructing proper scientific theories. Nevertheless, reports Capra (1972), the careful observation of nature, combined with a strong mystical intuition, led the Taoist sages to profound insights which are confirmed by modern scientific theories.

In general, Chinese thought has two complementary aspects: one that is practical and concerns itself with social consciousness, life in society, human relations, moral values and government; the other concerns itself more with one's mystical side, demanding that the highest aim of philosophy should be to transcend the world of society and everyday life to reach a higher plane of consciousness. Typically, the Chinese sage tries to unify the two complementary sides of human nature – intuitive wisdom with practical knowledge, and contemplation with social action. Confucianism was the philosophy of social organization, common sense and practical knowledge. It provided Chinese society with an educational system and with strict social conventions. Taoism was the philosophy which concerned itself with discovering the Way – although at the risk of obscuring maturity. One achieves happiness when one follows the natural order, acting spontaneously and trusting one's intuitive knowledge.

These two trends in Chinese thought are not in conflict. They are similar to the whole sense of Yin and Yang, that there is unity in opposites. In the Chinese view, all manifestations of the Tao are generated by the dynamic interplay of these two polar forces:

> *The* Yang *having reached its climax retreats in favor of the* Yin; *the* Yin *having reached its climax retreats in favor of the* Yang (Capra, 1975).

A familiar symbol depicting the dynamic character of *Yin* and *Yang* is called "T'ai-chi to," meaning Diagram of the Supreme Ultimate.

The diagram is a symmetric arrangement of the dark *Yin* and the bright *Yang*. The symmetry is rational, suggesting a continuous cyclic movement. The two dots symbolize the idea that each time one of the two forces reaches its extreme, it already contains in itself the seed of its opposite.

Being aware of this dynamic interplay is important in understanding the view that nothing is static, but rather that we live in a constant state of change. Learning the Tao means attuning oneself to the constant flow, becoming one with the flow. In its original cosmic sense, the Tao is the cosmic process in which all things are involved; the world is seen as a continuous flow and change. The seekers of the Way want to become "one with Tao," living in harmony with nature, seeking to know the patterns of the cosmic Way, characterized by coming and going, expansion and contraction.

The *I Ching* (Book of Changes) is used in Taoist practice both to predict the future and to discover the disposition of a present situation. It is highly recognized as a book of wisdom and broadly consulted. Jean Schinoda Bolin (1979), in *The Tao of Psychology: Synchronicity and the Self*, says the *I Ching* is a text that awakens us to an intuitive awareness of relationships hitherto unrecognized. The term synchronicity comes from Jung's idea that seemingly "coincidental" events that we cannot rationally explain can operate as messages to our conscious minds. *I Ching* predictions can do the same thing. Bolin (1979) says all intuitive impressions are important and maintains that effect is a necessary part of one's spiritual direction:

> To know how to choose a path with heart is to learn how to follow the inner beat of intuitive feeling. Logic can tell you superficially where a path might lead to, but it cannot judge whether your heart will be in it.

Many Westerners practice the *I Ching*. By casting yarrow sticks and interpreting meaning from the patterns revealed in the way they fall, practitioners believe that an understanding of the interplay between human insight and physical reality can be gained. By performing this ancient Chinese ritual, they accept it as intuitive guidance.

Harman and Rheingold (1984), in *Higher Creativity*, seek nothing short of new insights into spiritual power, says researcher Frank Barron: They tell about respondents in surveys they and others have conducted; survey participants describe an awareness of oneness with the universe and all its powers, of intimate relationships with the Earth and all its creatures, of a knowing-a gnosis related to that of the creator (or creative principle), and of a direct, unaided experience of unity.

Marilyn Ferguson (1980) quoted Zbigniew Brezinski, then chairman of the United States Security Council, when he spoke of an increasing yearning for something spiritual in advanced Western societies where materialism has proven unsatisfying:

> This is why there is a search for personal religion, for direct connection with the spiritual... Ultimately, every human being, once he reaches the stage of self-consciousness, wants to feel that there is some inner and deeper meaning to his existence than just being and consuming, and once he begins to feel that way, he wants his social organization to correspond to that feeling. This is happening on a world scale. We are engaged in an inner search for meaning.

References

Assagioli, R. (1965). *Psychosynthesis*. NY: The Viking Press.
Bolin, J. S. (1979). *The tao of psychology: synchronicity and the self*. San Francisco, CA: Harper & Row.
Capra, F. (1976). *The tao of physics*. NY: Bantam Books.
Ferguson, M. (1980). *The aquarian conspiracy*. Los Angeles, CA: Jeremy P. Tarcher, Inc.
Goldberg, P. (1983). *The intuitive edge*. Los Angeles, CA: Jeremy P. Tarcher, Inc.
Harman, W. & Rheingold, H. (1984). *Higher creativity: Liberating the unconscious for breakthrough insights*. Los Angeles, CA: Jeremy P. Tarcher, Inc.
Hastings, J. (1926). *The encyclopedia of religion and ethics*. United Kingdom: T. & T. Clark, Ltd.
Mitchell, E. (1986). Institute of Noetic Sciences Publication. Sausalito, CA.
Noddings, N. & Shire, P. J. (1984). *Awakening the inner eye: Intuition in education*. NY: Teachers College Press.
Suzuki, D. T. (1964). *An introduction to Zen Buddhism*. NY: Grove Press.
Vaughan, F. E. (1979). *Awakening intuition*. NY: Anchor Books.
Watts, A. (1962). *The joyous cosmology: Adventures in the chemistry of consciousness*. NY: Pantheon.

CHAPTER TEN

Accepting Your Intuitive Self

*This, above all,
to thine own self
be true . . .*

William Shakespeare
Hamlet

And now for the most important step: accepting your intuitive self. Making that acceptance is analogous to learning how to swim, for it requires letting go and trusting yourself. This "letting go" is easier said than done because any number of things can stand in the way. Among them are cultural and environmental blocks. Culture, as it is used here, is defined as the training and development we receive in what our society considers to be right or wrong and how we are expected to behave. In his book *Conceptual Blockbusting*, James L. Adams (1979), Associate Dean for Academic Affairs in the Stanford University School of Engineering, lists the following cultural blocks (particular to our culture) that stand in the way of exercising the creative or intuitive process:

1. Fantasy and reflection are a waste of time, lazy, even crazy.
2. Playfulness is for children only.
3. Problem-solving is a serious business and humor is out of place.
4. Reason, logic, numbers, utility, practicality are *good;* feeling, intuition, qualitative judgments, pleasure are *bad*.
5. Tradition is preferable to change.
6. Any problem can be solved by scientific thinking and lots of money.

Adams contends that environmental blocks are interrelated with the cultural blocks in that a lack of supportive environment often stands in the way of our expressing our intuition and creativity.

Notice number "4" in Adam's list of cultural blocks: good versus bad qualities. This notion has dominated Western culture and education throughout the centuries of our civilization. It is the "right-answer;" – it is the concept of "looking to authorities outside yourself for direction and solutions" to which many of us have been subjected and that, therefore, makes it difficult for us to "let go" and trust the inner self. So we do not take it lightly when we say, "Accept your intuitive self." With the information we've shared in this book, we hope that you have begun to appreciate the inner knowledge that is available to you. Appreciation of this precious human gift is a first step towards acceptance.

Valuing intuitive ability is apparently commonplace among those at the top of organizations or professions. One of the findings reported by Weston H. Agor in his book *Intuitive Management: Integrating Left and Right Management Skills* (1984) is that top management consistently score higher than other levels of management on an intuition scale. He stated:

> *Intuition appears to be a skill that is more prevalent as one moves up the management ladder. Top management in every* sample group tested scored higher than middle/lower managers in their *underlying ability* to use intuition to make decisions. It also appears that, the higher one goes in the level of government service (from county to national), the greater one's ability to use intuition . . . it appears plausible that one of the skills that top managers rely on most frequently is their intuitive ability to make the right decisions.

During 1981 and 1982 Agor tested managers across the country in a wide variety of organizational settings (business, government, education, military and health) at all levels of management responsibility and in various occupational specializations.

Similar findings were reported by Ned Herrmann, whose research in whole brain learning has been extensive. At a Whole Brain Learning Symposium in Key West (October 1987), Herrmann reported that people at the top of their professions and organizations trust and make more use of their intuitive abilities. Herrmann attributes the use of their intuition to their being visionaries who deal with long-range goals. They need to be able to think beyond immediate solutions, and they don't always have all of the factual data available to make short-range decisions. Therefore, situations they face often demand greater reliance on intuition. And, as has been said so often, intuitive ability increases with practice. The late J. P. Guilford, whose classic work has served as the foundation for subsequent research on human mental functioning, has said that any talent or skill must be practiced if it is to survive.

Agor, Herrmann and others suggest that you need to learn to risk using intuition to make decisions, and to learn from the process. Seek outside verification afterwards, and learn from your mistakes. Try making a decision intuitively about something in your life *right now,* for which the outcome won't produce dire consequences. Then check out the results analytically. Scientists, as we mentioned earlier, often proceed on hunches, verifying findings analytically at a later time. A simple way for you to start is to try guessing the correct time before looking at your watch or clock. By doing this, you can begin tuning into your inner clock. One friend of ours has gotten very good at this, and it's something that is easy to verify immediately.

Acceptance of your own inner knowledge can be further stimulated by paying attention to information that comes to you; sometimes, that information comes through dreams, as discussed earlier. Treat dreams as valuable sources of information from your unconscious. Begin to keep a record of their content, especially reoccurring ones. Note any patterns that may be developing.

In your thinking patterns, when ideas begin to flow, let them flow. Save any censoring, editing, or judging for later. Intuition doesn't evaluate. As Agor (1984) remarked:

> *It (intuition) indicates possibilities and provides insight into the nature of things. Ask yourself how many times you have had an inspiration or insight on how to solve a problem and then failed to follow upon it. Are you aware of how you close off the possible use of your intuition . . . ?*

Ray Bradbury, the famous science fiction writer, in a recent interview with Chris Harding (1987) said that as soon as an idea comes to him for a short story, he writes it down. He advises others to do the same, to act immediately on what comes intuitively, saving editing for later. Bradbury is addressing the same "go with the flow" advice that others give as well, that is, to be responsive to the intuitive processes.

In his autobiography *Mark It and Strike It* (1960), Steve Allen, a talented comedian and musician, talks about how his mind "delivers" many songs to him unbidden. *"Where melodies come from heaven only knows."* He goes on to say that, although he sometimes figures them out more or less mechanically at the piano, far more often he suddenly hears them in his mind without having made any conscious effort to call them into being:

> When I am brushing my teeth or driving to work or waking up in the morning I start to hum or whistle or even just think of a melody, and there it is. Another new song has been delivered to me from an unknown source.

You can learn a great deal about your own intuition by being aware of how it works for others, especially successful artists, scientists and business leaders. These individuals can serve to demonstrate that trusting intuition is rewarding. It may be difficult for you to exercise intuitive processes if you work in an environment that consistently operates in a logical, linear, sequential manner. Roberto Assagioli (1965), the founder of psychosynthesis (an approach of psychotherapy that stresses that each individual can direct the harmonious development of all aspects of personality), says:

> Intuition is one of the least recognized and least appreciated, and therefore one of the repressed or undeveloped (psychological) functions . . . Repression of intuition is produced by non-recognition, devaluation, neglect and lack of connection with other psychological functions.

Assagioli goes on to say that a major purpose of activating intuition is that of *"putting at the disposal of the individual a precious function which generally remains latent and unused, thereby leaving the individual incomplete in his or her development."* He stresses that intuition can be advocated by giving it attention, which has both feeding power and focusing power. In a sense, intuition has evocative power, and attention really implies appreciation and therefore valuation.

Even though your environment might not be as open as you'd like for you to experiment with intuitive decision-making, you owe it to yourself to make an effort to use intuition as much as you can. In a recent issue of the *New Age Journal,* Paul Winter, a musician lauded for his unique ability to be in tune with people and all forms of nature, discussed his tour of the Soviet Union. Winter's latest work (*Earthbeat*) is the first original music jointly created and recorded by Russians and Americans, specifically the Paul Winter Consort and the Dimitri Pokrovsky Singers, a popular traditional vocal group from Moscow. Rick Ingrasci (1988) in the *New Age* article "Consorting with Russians" states that the recording was a logical evolution of Winter's concept of "living music" whereby music serves as "a vital medium through which the cultural and national environments unite."

Winter described the Soviet audiences as among the most enthusiastic and appreciative he has ever played to. *"The people listen very deeply,"* he said. *"They listen with a depth of attention that I've found almost nowhere else in the world."* He suggests that when life is restricted, we may have to live in a more inner way. *"The Russian people have a profound love of beauty. Music is nourishment to their souls . . . "*

Allowing yourself to live in more inner ways means *risking*. Being attuned to and using your intuition may mean that you have to learn to take the risk of giving up some old comfortable ways of thinking and doing things, of giving up the security of "proven" ways. It is this personal stretching that allows you to utilize what many times you know you knew anyway! In an article in *Personal Computing* called "The Well-Tempered Risk," Evan Peele (1982) makes the point that risk takers are optimistic, positive thinkers and they expect to be successful:

> . . . *research shows that risk takers are usually the most successful people. They tend to be effective on the job, leaders in their fields, and highest in management ranks. They also attain higher income and profit levels while experiencing the least stress.*

Intuition, your inner knowing, is there for you to make use of. It is valued in all aspects of human life. Theologian and artist Catherine A. Kapikian in an interview by Linda Monk (1988) in *Common Boundary,* responded in this way to the question "What made you decide to go to seminary in the first place? Was it a sense that creativity and spirituality were somehow related?":

> *I knew, in an intuitive sense, that they were related because the process of creativity, of that private time in my studio trying to create or discover a solution, was the time I always felt closest to my Creator . . . It was a meditating time . . . I knew deep inside me that it was the most valuable expenditure of my time . . .*

Dave Cornish and Ed Moloney work for Vollmer Associates, an engineering firm responsible for keeping the operations underneath the streets of New York running. Donald Dale Jackson (1987) in a *Smithsonian* article said these two men, along with their boss Arnold Vollmer, are authorities on the workings of underground Manhattan, specialists in the tangled thicket of pipes, conduits, mains, tunnels, tubes, ducts and cables that wind beneath the streets and keep it humming. Moloney remarked, "From our experience and what we've learned in the trenches, we have a kind of sixth sense of what we're likely to run into down there." Cornish said, "A manhole tells you where a line is but not which way it goes, and a lot of time you're working by feel and intuition."

Nobel-prize-winning particle physicist Murray Gell-Mann makes a plea for artists and scientists alike to employ both the rational and intuitive approach. In an article in *Science News,* Stefi Weisburd (1987) reported on a symposium at the Smithsonian Institution where artists and scientists gave personal testimonies concerning their creativity. A number of the participants reported that they first prepare their minds with pertinent information, and then allow the intuitive response to "float to the top" toward the solution of discovery. However, often it does take a long time, as in the work of Linus Pauling, who discovered the medicinal properties of Vitamin C. He shared that one solution of his – the alpha-helix structure – took nineteen years from the time he learned the necessary factual information to the achievement of the actual solution, and then, the solution occurred while he was lying in bed with a cold.

Rosalyn Turick, a renowned concert artist, has discovered new insights into Bach's music. She states that it took two years of concentrated study of Bach prior to her first insight, and that one does not receive such intuitive experiences out of nothing.

Each one of us has within ourselves an accumulated knowledge that is the result of collective, universal knowledge and a unique personal knowledge that has been gained through experience. This knowledge is there, waiting to be tapped.

Accept the gift that is yours for the taking. Accept your intuitive self.

References

Adams, J. L. (1979). *Conceptual blockbusting.* NY: W. W. Norton and Company.
Agor, W. H. (1984). *Intuitive management: Integrating left and right management skills.* Englewood Cliffs, NJ: Prentice-Hall.
Allen, S. (1960). *Mark it and strike it.* NY: Holt, Rinehart & Winston.
Assagioli, R. (1965). *Psychosynthesis.* NY: Viking Press.

Browning, D. C. (1986). *The complete dictionary of Shakespeare quotations.* United Kingdom: New Orchard Editions.

Harding, C. (1987). *Omni audio experience, premiere issue.* Interview with Ray Bradbury. Bonneville Communications in collaboration with Omni Publications International, Ltd.

Ingrasci, R. (1988). Consorting with Russians. *New Age Journal, 4* (1).

Jackson, D. D. (1987). It takes a 'sixth sense' to operate underneath the streets of New York. *Smithsonian, 18* (5), 39-46.

Monk, L. (1988). Radical trust in the creative process: An interview with Catherine A. Kapikian. *The Common Boundary, 6* (1), 7-9.

Peele, E. (1982). The well-tempered risk. *Personal Computing, 6* (7), 28-30.

Weisburd, S. (1987). The spark: Personal testimonies of creativity. *Science News, 132* (Nov.), 298-300.

Index

A

Active imagination, 57
Adams, James L., 101-102
Age regression, 59-60
Agnew, Harman W., 14
Agor, Weston H., 10, 16, 18-19, 103
Ahsen, Akhter, 10, 17-18, 65
Allen, Steve, 103-104
Aquinas, Thomas, 92
Arieti, Silvano, 53
Aristotle, 2
Assagioli, Roberto, 62, 92, 104
Assessing intuition, 17-23
    Ahsen Age Projection Test, 17-18
    Eidetic Parents Test, 18
    Shorr Imagery Test, 18
    Agor Intuitive Scale, 18-19
    Goldberg's Intuitive Powers, 19-23
Autogenic training, 33, 63

B

Bamberger, Jeanne, 42
Banting, Sir Frederick Grant, 68
Bastick, Tony, 7
Bechman, Max, 52
Beck, Aaron T., 58
Bergenthal, James, 5
Bohm, David, 74-75
Bohr, Niels, 68
Bolin, Jean Schinoda, 99
Bradbury, Ray, 103
Brahms, Johannes, 51
Breuer, Joseph, 56
Brezinski, Zbigniew, 99
Bronowski, Jacob, 35
Bruner, Jerome, 42, 48, 71-72
Brunton, Paul, 9

Buddha, 2
Budzynski, Thomas H., 10, 12

C

Capra, Fritjof, 53, 75, 97-98
Ch'an philosophy, 97-98
Chaos, 81
Children and intuition, 41-48
Christianity, 85
Clark, Barbara, 44-46
Cocteau, Jean, 51
Cognitive therapy, 59
Color therapies, 86
Corsini, Raymond J., 65
Court, Simon, 10, 11, 15, 16
Creation, 80
Creation goddesses, 80-83
    Gaia, 81
    Yemaya, 82
    Spider Woman, 82
    Ishatar, 83
Creative arts, 49-54
Creative visualization, 39-40, 86-87
Creativity and intuition, 7-8
Crick, Francis, 75-76
Crystals, 86-87
Csikszentmihalyi, Mihaly, 9

D

DaEl, 86
Dean, Douglas, 15
Descartes, 70
Developing and increasing intuition, 25-40
Directed imagery, 64-65
Discovery intuition, 6
Dreams, 31-32, 57-58, 68-71

E

Eidetic imagery therapy, 65-66
Eidetic Parents Test and Analysis, 65

Einstein, Albert, 67, 73-74
Emerson, Ralph Waldo, 1
Ernst, Max, 49-50
Esalen Institute, 91
Evaluation intuition, 6

F

Fausto-Sterling, Anna, 79
Ferguson, Marilyn, 12, 89, 94-95, 99-100
Forward time projection, 58
Freud, Sigmund, 55-57
Functional types of intuition, 6-7
Futures wheel of the problem, 27

G

Gaia, 81-82
Gauss, Johann F. K., 72-73
Gawain, Shakti, 39-40
Gell-Mann, Murray, 106
Gemstones, 87
Gestalt therapy, 64
Glenn, Jerry, 27
Goldberg, Philip, 6-7, 10, 19-23, 74, 92-93
Goldberg, Steven, 80
Goldfried, Marvin R., 59
Gonzales-Wippler, Migene, 82
Gowan, John C., 8, 51
Greeks, 1, 82
Greeley, Andrew, 10, 12
Guided affective imagery, 61-62

H

Happich, Carl, 60
Harman, Willis W., 30-31, 88-89, 91, 99
Healing and gemstones, 87
    psychic, 86

Hemisphericity, 38-40
Hermann, Ned, 38-39, 102
Hildegarde of Bingen, 85
Hinduism, 2, 96
Hologram, 74
Howe, Elias, 68
Hunter god, 83-84
Hutchinson, Eliot D., 35

I

I Ching, 99
Idealism, 2
Illumination intuition, 7
Imagery, 35-38, 67-71
Implosive therapy, 59
Induced dreams, 57-58
The Institute of Transpersonal Psychology, 94
Integration therapy, 64
Intuition
    and incubation, 5
    blocks to, 101
    children and, 41-48
    creative arts and, 49-54
    creativity and, 7-8
    cultural and historical context, 8
    definition of, 1, 2-4, 8
    development of, 25
    dreams and, 31-32
    flow and, 10
    imagery and, 6
    imaging techniques and, 35-37
    in business, 15-16
    levels of intuitive awareness, 3-6
    mathematics and, 72-73
    meaning of, 1-23
    music and, 104-105
    psychology and, 55-66
    rationality and, 1-2
    relaxation and, 32-33
    research and, 9-10
    risk and, 103-105
    sciences and mathematics, 67-77
    scientific models and, 9
    seers and oracles, 1
    stimulating, 25-26
    tests and instruments, 17-23
    types of, 6-7
    visualization techniques and, 35-38
    women's, 79-90
Intuitive modes, 34-35, 50-52
Ishatar, 83

J

Jacobson, Edmund, 59
Jaensch, Erich R., 65
Jones, Rufus, 92
Judaism, 84
Judeo-Christian philosophy, 96
Jung, Carl G., 2-3, 10, 16, 28, 50, 52, 75, 77, 99

K

Kapikian, Catherine A., 105
Kegan, Robert, 44
Kekule von Stradonitz, August, 69
Klee, Paul, 52
Knowlson, T. Sharper, 34-35

L

LaBerge, Stephen, 10, 13, 31-32
Laing, Ronald D., 64
LeCron, Leslie M., 59
Leuner, Hanscarl, 62
Levels of intuitive awareness, 3
    physical level, 3
    emotional level, 4
    mental level, 4-5
    spiritual level, 5-6
Levis, Donald J., 59
Lindemann, Hannes, 63
Loewi, Otto, 69
Lutke, Wolfgang, 33

M

MacKinnon, Donald W., 7-8, 47
Mahoney, Michael J., 59
Maltz, Maxwell, 30
Mariechild, Diane, 87
Maslow, Abraham, 12, 53, 87, 93, 94, 95-96
Mathematicians, 71-73
McCready, William, 10, 12
Meditation, 14-15, 32
Mendeleev, Dimitrie I., 68
Mihalsky, John, 10, 15-16
Mill, John Stuart, 79-80
Mitchell, Edgar, 74, 93
Mozart, Wolfgang Amadeus, 50
Muir, Jane, 70
Murphy, Michael, 91-92
Music and intuition, 104-105
Myers, Frederic W., 55-56
Mystical and intuitive experiences, 11-14

N

Newton, Isaac, 74
Noddings, Nel, 1, 2, 96
Noetics Institute, 93
Norman, Donald, 4

O

Operation intuition, 7
Ornstein, Robert E., 39
Ouseley, G. S. J., 86

P

Pascal, Blaise, 72
Patriarchy, 84-85

Pauling, Linus, 106
Pearce, Joseph Chilton, 4, 46
Peele, Evan, 105
Perls, Fritz, 64
Poincare, Henri, 73
Prediction intuition, 7
Pribram, Karl, 74
Principles of cognition, 10-11
Psychic healing, 86
Psycho-imagination theory, 64
Psychology and intuition, 55
Puccini, Giacomo, 51
Pure consciousness, 93

R

Ramanujan, 72
Reason, 6
Reflexology, 85
Reingold, Howard, 30-31, 88-89, 91, 99
Relaxation, 32-33
Roberts, Jane, 88
Romans, 1
Rudhyar, Dane, 52
Russell, Bertrand, 73

S

Sacerdote, Paul, 57
Salk, Jonas, 43, 74
Samuels, Mike, 70
Samuels, Nancy, 70
Satori, 97
Schucman, Helen, 88
Schultz, Johannes H., 33
Scientists, 67-72, 73-77
Seed thought, 17
Self-image theory, 64-65
Sensing, 3
Seth, 88
Shepherd, Roger, 35
Sherman, Julia A., 80
Shore, Paul, 1, 2, 96

Shorr, Joseph E., 10, 18, 36-37, 64-65
Simonton, Dean K., 7
Singer, Jerome, 10, 13-14
Sinnott, Edmund W., 71
Sitwell, Edith, 52
Sorokin, Pitirim A., 68
Sound pondering, 17
Spearman, Charles E., 9-11
Spider Woman, 82-83
Spinoza, Baruch, 5
Spirituality, 91-92
   and intuition, 91-100
   women and, 89
Spontaneous imagery, 64-65
Spretnak, Charlene, 81
Stampfl, Thomas G., 59
Stein, Diane, 81, 86
Fausto-Sterling, Anne, 79-80
Stone, Merlin, 84
Suedfeld, Peter, 11
Sullivan, Harry Stack, 64
Superstring theory, 76-77
Symbolic consciousness, 60-61
Symbolic visualization, 62-63
Systematic desensitization, 58-59

T

Talamonti, Leo, 68
Taoism, 75, 97, 98
Tesla, Nikola, 69-70
Three principles of cognition, 10
Transcendence, 92-95
Transpersonal education, 94-95
Transpersonal psychology, 94-95
Turick, Rosalyn, 106

U

Unconscious, 55-56
Understanding and assessing intuition, 9-23
Universal symbols, 84
Urban, Walter, 64

V

Vaughn, Frances E., 3, 5, 49, 93
Visualization techniques, 35-38, 55-66
Vollmer Associates, 105

W

Waters, Frank, 82
Watson, James, 75
Watts, Alan, 96
Webb, Wilse B., 14
Weisburd, Stefi, 106
Winter, Paul, 104
Witten, Edward, 76-77
Wolpe, Joseph, 58
Women as healers, 85-86
Women's intuition, 79-90

Y

Yellot, John, 71
Yemaya, 82
Yin and Yang, 98
Yoga, 2, 5-6, 33-34

Z

Zen Buddhism, 96-97
Zen meditation, 2
Zen philosophy, 53, 96-97

Other Books . . .

Leadership: Making Things Happen
Dorothy A. Sisk & Doris J. Shallcross
ISBN 0-943456-16-9

This book is designed to help clarify the meaning of leadership and to develop and strengthen leadership skills. The content is based on two major premises: the first is that leaders do not function alone, but operate in a context in which they are involved with other people; the second is that each person must be the dynamic force behind their own growth.

Leadership: Making Things Happen combines the best of the traditional and innovative approaches to leadership training in looking at the "whole person's" development. It still may be that there are "born leaders"; but if it is also possible to train one, this book will figure heavily in such a process.

The Growing Person:
How To Encourage Healthy
Emotional Development In Children
Doris J. Shallcross & Dorothy A. Sisk
ISBN 0-943456-06-1

A guide for parents and teachers on how to help children become emotionally well adjusted. This book contains dozens of stimulating and effective activities that can be used to help children better understand and accept their emotional lives.

Complete with exercises that can be easily adapted for one or more children, this book reveals many things that you need to know to help children lead emotionally healthy lives, including critical information on how to: understand how children develop their self-concepts; assess your child's emotional maturity; teach children to express their emotions in a constructive manner; encourage children to accept responsibility for their own lives; help children give and receive emotional support; increase your child's self-awareness through social interaction; motivate children to become more self-directed; help children develop accurate interpretive skills; and much more.

Teaching Creative Behavior: How To Evoke Creativity In Children Of All Ages

Doris J. Shallcross
ISBN 0-943456-07-X

An important classroom handbook that encourages creative behavior on the part of both the teacher and the student and describes optimal conditions for creative teaching and learning. This valuable guide can be used to motivate students or learners of all ages to derive a sense of fulfillment through exploration of their own creative potentials.

The reader will discover helpful classroom strategies for guiding the individual student or students in groups and setting the mental, emotional, and physical climate for creativity. There are dozens of activities that develop students' sensitivity and awareness, along with techniques that help students focus on the real problems before them and the real goals to be achieved. Finally, specific practical directions are offered for the teacher seeking to evoke a greater proportion of creative student behavior in the classroom.

Orders or inquiries should be addressed to

BEARLY LIMITED
149 York Street
Buffalo, New York 14213